Stories of Awe and Abundance

Sr. José Hobday, OSF

continuum
NEW YORK • LONDON

2006

The Continuum International Publishing Group Inc
80 Maiden Lane, New York, NY 10038

Printed in the United States of America

Library of Congress Cataloging-in-Publication Data

Hobday, José
    Stories of awe and abundance / José Hobday.
        p.   cm.
    ISBN 0-8264-1161-4
    1. Hobday, José.   2. Spiritual life—Catholic Church.   I. Title.
    [BX4705.H6333A3   1999]
    248.4'82—dc21   99-11600
                                                                                    CIP

These stories have been taken from *Praying* magazine, edited by Art Winter

Contents

In gratitude to my family
and every person who has done good to me,
whether known or unknown,
in hard times and easy times.

Prayers Made for Walking

I like to pray when I walk. In good weather I have walked as far as three or four miles in prayer. I will read some scripture or an excerpt from a notebook that I keep, and then I walk. Sometimes, too, I will spend a longer period of time in silence before I start walking. In that way I combine the two – silent, still prayer and walking prayer.

In spring and summer I frequently pray while walking in cemeteries. I got in the habit of doing that in Arizona, where it is dry and there isn't much grass, except in the cemeteries which are watered and maintained. As a result I learned to pray with the dead. That's a great way of praying – in the presence of the dead. The cemetery I walked in was green and grassy. It was all mine. Rarely did anybody invade my meditation place.

When I combine the two ways of praying – being quiet first and then walking – I do what I think of as walking the prayer into my body. Let's say I reflected quietly on a beautiful image from nature. A glorious sunrise would be an example. As I walk I keep that image in front of me, and, after a while, I have a strong sense of the sunrise, of light, inside of me. That's what I mean by walking the image into my body.

Usually I make the time in silent prayer brief. Most often, before walking I will recall a favorite scripture story and re-explore it as I go. I use some stories over and over. One is from the Book of Kings, the story of Elijah and Elisha, his disciple. I like it because it tells a story of friendship in which people become the source of strength for one another.

Elijah was a great prophet who confronted the errors of his time in an effective way. This impressed Elisha and he asked if he could become his disciple. After Elisha worked with Elijah for a while, Elijah let him know he would be leaving him, because the Lord was about to take him up into heaven in a whirlwind. Elisha wanted to learn everything he could from Elijah, who was not only his mentor but his friend. So, Elisha said, "Let me walk with you wherever you go."

Finally, when it was about time to go, Elijah said, "Is there anything you would like to ask of me as a gift?" Elisha, who already had in mind what he wanted, said, "Yes, I would like a double portion of your spirit." What a thing to say! Imagine loving someone that much! Elijah said, "I don't know if I can promise you that, but if you see me going up into heaven, leaving you, then you know you have the gift." When Elisha saw Elijah taken up in a fiery chariot, he knew he had the gift. And then he walked in the power of Elijah's spirit.

In going back over that story, I think about how wonderful it would be to have a double portion of another person's spirit, say, Teresa of Avila, or Francis, or Clare. When I walk in a cemetery I think about all the people buried there and all their power and goodness, and I feel strengthened, as if I had received their spirit in the same way that Elisha received Elijah's. Because of our belief in the communion of saints, I believe that actually happens. I believe when I walk in the dust of people who have died, yearning for a portion of their spirit, some of their spirit actually comes to me.

Sometimes, too, I will walk with my name, José. I love my name. It comes from Joseph, meaning "God keeps adding" or "God increases." When I walk with my name I say something like this to God, "Increase in me. That's what I am here for. Let it happen. That's what my name means and that's what I want to happen."

At other times I walk and pray with my Dad or Mom. They had their faults, as all parents do, but they were extraordinarily beautiful people. Walking in the memory of how much they shared with us, with me, helps me to see that I have some of the beauty they had. It gives me the strength they had. They believed their beauty and strength came from God, and recalling that in my walking prayer, helps me to see that mine does too.

Walking prayer brings home that God always walks with me, with us. God walked with Adam and Eve in the garden. God

2

walked among us in Jesus the Son. And God walks among us now in the Spirit. And that is true whether we are walking or not, whether we are praying or not.

Stories My Mom and Dad Taught Me

2

No one influenced my prayer and spirituality more than my mother and dad. My mother taught me to pray in a playful way. As a result I love to play with God, as if I were a child playing with my parents. I like going to a playground, getting in a swing and swinging high, because I believe God lives in us through the joy and power we sense when we swing high.

I like flying kites because it is such a wild, freeing thing. I think God works within lifted spirits. That is true, I think, of any kind of play – running, roller skating, rolling in the leaves, just kicking around and making noise, wasting time, having a party. I still believe God is present in those playful moments, just as my mother taught me.

I try to pass this sense of the sacred in playfulness on to children. Right now, there's a three-year-old girl living next door to me. Every time I see her, she smiles, giggles and runs into my arms. I hug her and she runs away – and then she runs back into my arms again. Since we started doing that, it strikes me as a wonderful image of prayer – running into God's arms. One of these days, I will begin making the connection for her.

But back to my parents. My parents' influence goes back not only to what they did but to the stories they told me about their lives. My father grew up as a very religious person in the hard-shell Southern Baptist tradition. Son of a minister, he found it a rather harsh way to live because you couldn't smoke, gamble, drink, dance or play cards. One day, while reading the gospels as a teenager, it struck him that Jesus hung around with people who did these kinds of things. After shopping around, he decided to join the Catholic church, because he saw more riffraff there than in any other church. He saw that as a good sign Jesus would be hanging around there. I love that story.

My mother, who was raised in the Native American tradition, attended an Indian school for a time. After her parents died a Lutheran family adopted her. When she met my father, Lutherans did not like Catholics much, and her family told her that if she married him, she should be dead as far as they were concerned. My mother knew that was not the right attitude and she went ahead and married him.

Here's another of my favorite family stories. It goes back to weeks after my mother and father were married. It concerns my mother's long black hair. One day – and remember this was in 1919 – my father came home from work talking about women he had seen who had cut off their long hair. They looked like plucked chickens, he said. He went on about these women and what he would do if his wife cut her hair. Without saying anything my mother went out the next day and had her hair cut off. That night when my father came home and saw her he cried. He couldn't believe it.

My mother sat him down at the table and said, "John, I love you more than anything in the world, but I am not my hair. I am my own person. And don't ever again say what you would do if your wife does such and such. You consult with me." My Dad said, "You know how much I loved your hair." And she said, "Yes, and if you want it, go get it. It's down the street at the beauty shop." And just to show what kind of man he was, he went and got it.

My mother's cutting her hair symbolized freedom. It showed her as her own person. This happened in a time when men made the decisions – women, for example, did not even have the right to vote. My mother came out of a strong matriarchal tradition. My father had come from a totally different one, a southern mentality in which men sat around and women waited on them. Later, my Dad would say, "Your mother was my freedom. I learned freedom from her."

This story meant freedom for me, too. My mother's swatch of hair remained in our house as a sign of freedom from traditional

5

sex roles. It became a clear sign to my brothers that I, as the only girl in the family, was nobody's slave. When my father died we buried my mother's hair with him because it was such an important part of his story. It struck me as a good symbol for the new freedom he now enjoyed in Christ.

My parents told me many stories like these. They were stories of understanding, growth, forgiveness. In short, they were love stories. They were based on spiritual values. They involved choices for God. When I was young, I never got tired of hearing these stories. When Mom and Dad were telling stories, I always wished they would not stop, that the stories would never end. And it turns out they have not, for they have become part of my story.

The Treasure in the Desert

3

One Saturday morning when I was in the seventh grade, I waited for my friend, Juanita, to come over to play. As usual she did not arrive on time. I started griping. Why does she always have to be late? The more time passed, the worse I got until I finally I reached the downright obnoxious stage. Finally my father had enough.

"Jo," he said, "get a book, an apple and a blanket, and get in the car." I said, "No, I'm not going, Juanita's coming." My mother, apparently knowing what Dad was up to, said, "Do as your father tells you. I'll take care of Juanita."

Dad drove me out to a spot in the desert near a canyon. "Get out," he said. "We can't stand you around the house. We don't want to live with you anymore. You stay down here by yourself all day – until you can figure out how to be decent around other people when things aren't going your way."

I got out of the car. He threw my things out after me. Now I really fumed. Daddy didn't usually treat me this way, because, as his only daughter, I had become what you might call a pet. I shouted at him: "Now I know I'm adopted. Otherwise, you wouldn't treat me this way." He just said, "I'll be back for you tonight," and drove off. I fumed some more, and before I finished I had thrown my apple, book, blanket over the edge of the canyon.

I spent eight or nine hours there alone. After the first hour or so, I settled down. At noon, I climbed down and got my things and ate the apple. I spent the longest time lying under a tree. Gradually I came to terms with what had happened. I got rid of the anger and all the hostile feelings I had. Finally I could see my behavior wasn't what it should be and that Dad was right.

I felt better, but my sense of being alone increased. Why hadn't Juanita come? Oh, how I wish she were her with me. When my loneliness reached the point where I could hardly stand it, it seemed to ease. I started feeling a kind of presence. I seemed less alone. In time, I came to believe I had an experience of God coming to me. With that came a tremendous sense of God's love for me. Lying under that tree, I saw the world as beautiful and I felt wonderful about being out in it by myself.

It was a contemplative experience – my first, but not my last. In fact, it led to living in the world as a contemplative, as one who senses God everywhere, as one who feels loved by God any time, anywhere. In that way, this experience proved a wonderful gift. I got another gift as well – honesty. Once I looked at my behavior honestly, I could see Daddy was not only right, but that he did what he did for my own good.

When he came to get me, we made up – right away. I shall never forget this experience. It gave me a taste for the spiritual that comes only through solitude. Often I think this experience lay at the heart of my religious vocation. I believe I felt I could take the huge risk of living without an intimate human relationship because I had found something profoundly intimate in that experience of solitude.

After the experience, I would take a day off – usually every month during the summer – and go by myself to the same place where Daddy had dropped me off. I would have the same experience. I just sat and waited for it. It wasn't anything overwhelming or extraordinary. I just had a profound sense of being held in God.

I regard it as the great gift for my life, my treasure in the field, my pearl of great price. For years and years, I have kept going on the power that it gives me. It never leaves. When I go off by myself I always relive the day that Juanita didn't come, but God did.

The Ice Cream that Set Me Free

4

I tell this story often. I do so because it strikes me as a real gospel story. It is my strawberry ice cream story.

This happened when I was a child, on a Saturday night. I was doing my homework in the front room. My brothers played outside. My dad and mom talked in the kitchen, about money. I couldn't make out all they said, but it seemed as if they were figuring out how much we had to live on for the next week. And I had no doubt about one thing: There wasn't much.

As the conversation in the kitchen continued I became anxious. I suspected that we might not have enough money for food for the next week. My mother was trying to hold back a little for necessities, but dad kept pointing out how they had not paid the bills, first this one, then that one. Finally, at a point when I began to get pretty uptight about this, my mother walked into the living room and put three or four dollars down in front of me. "Honey," she said, "go get some your of brothers and go to the drug store and buy some strawberry ice cream."

I knew we didn't have money to waste so I ran back to Daddy and said, "Did you hear what Momma told me to do? To take all the money we've got to live on and spend it on ice cream?" I remember him looking at me and saying, "Honey, your Momma is right. When we start worrying this much about a few dollars, we are better off having nothing at all. Go get your brothers and go buy the ice cream."

I did. And in those days three or four dollars would buy a lot of ice cream. We brought back big brown bags of it. My mother put on the record player, opened the doors and invited the neighbors. She set out bowls and spoons on the table and everybody gathered around, including all the kids in the neighborhood, and we ate up all the ice cream and had a good time.

I don't remember what we did for money or for food the next week, but I will never forget the party we had that night. To me, it seemed a real response to the scriptures: "Look at the birds of the air and the lilies of the field. They don't sow or spin and your Father looks after them." Going out and buying the strawberry ice cream represented a kind of flinging ourselves into the arms of God. I still live off that experience, and, as a result, I don't worry much about money.

I try to live on God's providence and people's goodness. Believe me, it's as exciting as the gospel says. As I have flown around the country speaking on prayer and spirituality, I have tried to teach people to live this way. I try to get people to discover how freeing this can be – to see what happens when they don't have credit cards or big bank accounts.

What happens, for example, when you sleep in airports?

In my travels, I have slept in enough airports to know what happens. Very often, the cleaning people go and get you blankets. That's what happens. Great things happen, blessed encounters take place when you throw yourself on God's mercy and peoples' kindness. I find it very exciting. It's sad that Christians don't know how freeing it is to get loose from material things. It is different from being poor because you are poor. Poverty can be a curse, but choosing it can be the greatest gift. It can set you free.

Sometimes when I talk like this, I get this response: "It's easy for you to talk about money in this way, Sister José, because you are a religious sister, you don't have children to support, etc." That is true. Of course, couples and families must concern themselves with feeding and housing and educating themselves and their children. What I'm saying is this: Look at your tendencies to consume and to store instead of sharing. Look at your tendencies to find security in things instead of trusting in the Lord.

My parents, after all, had a house full of children. In buying the ice cream, they decided to be thankful for the little they had and to celebrate it. In doing so, they chose not to worry about the fact that they didn't have more, and to trust that God and

God's creation would provide. I am glad they decided to buy the ice cream. Not only was it delicious, but it gave me a taste for freedom.

The Native American Way: Praying by Doing

5

My mother prayed as a Native American. That meant she saw living as praying and praying as living. She tried to pray her life. She expressed her prayer of gratitude, for example, in the way she did things. She told me many times, "When you stir oatmeal, stir it slowly so you don't forget that oatmeal is a gift and that you don't take it for granted."

She made a prayer out of the way she stirred oatmeal. Doing things prayerfully. That reflected her approach to prayer. She always did that. She even did it in the way she walked. She taught me and my brothers to walk with our hearts high and to walk softly on the earth because the earth is our mother. As a result, everyone in our family walked proudly and softly – and prayerfully.

As we walked, she said, we should be ready to enter into every movement of beauty we encountered. Meanwhile, our feet should not crush the earth but walk lightly. Like all Native Americans, my mother was a nature person. Like many Native Americans, she liked living outside as much as possible. She was no house potato. When I was a child, I went out in every kind of weather. We did not live in houses that were excessively warm. When it snowed my mother would say, "Go out and play in the snow. Go out and love the snow. It will only be here for a little while, so don't miss it." When it rained, she said, "Go walk in the rain. Feel it."

The Native American tradition contains profoundly Christian values. These values are profoundly American, too, in that they come from this land. As American Christians, we must explore these. Thomas Merton said that until you explore the Native

American tradition, you will never be an American. You will always be an import.

So, what things have I learned from Native American spirituality? First, to make my prayer creation-centered. Indians pray as relatives of the earth. They consider the sky their father, the earth their mother. The sun can be a brother or a sister. This makes you a creature with a relationship to creation, not someone above it or better than it.

Now, we can assault creation because we think of ourselves as superior. But you and I are not superior to the earth or its creatures. Take ants, for example They help keep the soil porous. They protect plants. They don't violate the earth as we humans do. In our prayer, we might very well reflect on ants and other creatures, and their relationship with creation. That is what Native Americans have done. It has not only kept them in touch with creation, but with the Creator as well.

Second, I have learned a great sense of the dead from Native Americans. As a Catholic I believe in the communion of saints but Native Americans have a sense of the dead that is a way of life. The keep alive the memory of people who have died by telling their stories. This affects how they view death and how they live. Since they know others will celebrate their memories when they are gone, they fear death less and live more joyfully.

Third, I have learned about silence from Native Americans. They have learned to love and respect silence, to cherish solitude, to spend time alone. For them, and I think for all of us, the best solitude is out in nature. Nothing can beat noticing nature's peaceful elements – breezes, water, sunshine, grasses, flowers. Fourth, living in harmony is another Native American spiritual value. In order not to be at war with yourself, you must be in harmony with the earth, with your ancestors, and with your own vision and faith.

Finally, Native Americans value celebration. Dance when you can, party when you can. That's their tradition. If there is no reason to celebrate, find a reason. Indians joke that they spend the whole summer on the powwow trail. Actually they aren't just celebrating and partying. They are keeping spiritual values alive, and they do it by dancing and singing and visiting and going all out for beauty and pleasure. Keeping spiritual values alive through these activities makes them prayers, doesn't it? Like my mother's, these prayers are prayers of doing. If you would like to try praying by doing, I suggest stirring your oatmeal – slowly – as a good way to begin.

A God of Awe and Abundance

6

In my life I have gotten to know a very loving, personal, caring, creative and almost capricious God. Sometimes when I talk with people I have a tremendous sense that God is just revealing who God is through that person. Good people give me an image of the goodness of God, the creativity of God, the patience of God.

I have an image of God who is so forgiving and so loving that I have never – no matter what I have done – felt outside of God. I have never felt that I had done anything so bad that I was no longer welcome, that I had to keep my distance. Largely as a result of my parents' influence, my image of God includes a sense of justice. They felt you should acknowledge the things you did wrong and make up for them.

I have experienced God as friend and teacher, as lover and beloved, and when I know I have been off target, as judge, though never as a harsh one. Mostly perhaps, God is a companion. I have a wonderful image of God as goodness and beauty. I know when I am looking at flowers that they are God's reflection. I know when I experience love that God is love. Sometimes I get a sense of God as vitality within me. It is a very personal wholeness and sense of reverence.

How does this image of God fit in with all the pain and suffering in the world? I have learned much from the Native American attitude toward suffering and death. My mother used to put it this way: "Until you can put your arms around all of life, which includes death and dying, you will never really understand life."

Death is part of life. Seasons die. Ideas die. Leaves die. People die. Everything has a life-death cycle. That fits right in with Christ's message: Unless you die, unless you fall into the ground, you cannot have new life. Unless you go to the cross with Jesus, you do not have resurrection and fullness of life.

I really believe Jesus' words that "I have come that you may have life and have it to the full." The gospels are full of stories in which it looks as if people will be overwhelmed by things. And what is Jesus' response? He says that love is the way through such things. That's what gives you life to the hilt.

For me, faith in God, and especially in Jesus Christ, helps in discovering this about life. Faith helps me to make connections and to see things more clearly. It helps me to see the basic paradox Jesus leads us to – that death leads to life, that the grain of wheat must die, that one who lays down his life shows the greatest love. This leads to abundant life. Without faith this remains difficult to see.

Faith is like a shift key on a typewriter. You can type along in lower case and you have exactly the same message as you would have if you hit the shift key and started typing in all capital letters. But when you hit the shift key, everything is brighter and cleaner and bolder and easier to see.

With faith, I have come to know a God who is creative.

God has become an exciting God for me. The more I see God in all things, the more I find I am called to respond. I can almost hear God say, "Be still and find out that I am God. Look and let yourself be amazed. Be quiet and experience reverence. Quit counting what you think you're worth and let me overwhelm you with love."

I have tried to do that – be still and let God overwhelm me with love. When I do, I find myself responding with reverence, silence, amazement, awe, gratitude, delight.

For me God has become a God of awe. God is a God of abundance. Like many Christians before me, I have tried to share this experience with people. And like so many before, I have found stories the best way to do that. Not surprisingly, they are stories of awe and abundance.

The Sacrifice Flower

7

My mother, who was a Native American, taught me all kinds of wonderful ways to pray when I was a child. A very special one was the Sacrifice Flower prayer, which she adapted from the heritage of her people, the Seneca Iroquois. She taught me to say this prayer when I was feeling low or had a burden I wanted lifted. Later, I learned to use it for happy occasions and when I had a special request I wanted to make of God.

Like all mothers, she could always tell when something was bothering me. She'd say to me, "All right, Jo. I think it's time you went outside and found yourself a Sacrifice Flower. It's time you get your burden lifted from your heart and give it to God."

So, I would go looking for a flower. Sometimes Mother would go out with me to help me with my flower or talk about what was bothering me. Sometimes, too, she had something weighing on her heart and she would find a Sacrifice Flower of her own.

That flower was supposed to be special, one that meant a lot to me. As a girl, I picked dandelions, hollyhocks, and daisies. So I usually picked one of them. In addition, Mother said I was to be very careful with the flower because it had been selected for a holy purpose. I lovingly cupped it in my hands so nothing would happen to it.

When I got home, I did as my mother instructed and told the flower what burden I wanted lifted and taken to God. How was the flower to do this? Remember, this was a Sacrifice Flower, one that was going to die. The idea was that as life went out of the flower, it would carry my prayer to God.

That meant, of course, the flower was not to be placed in water. I had a shelf in my room that I liked to use for my Sacrifice

Flower because it was sort of private and yet I could see it as I went in and out.

Every time I saw the flower, I could see it giving its life for me and I could imagine my prayer being carried to God. That was true even when I was elsewhere and was just thinking about the flower. Either way, I had a strong sense my prayer was being heard. My flower and I were in union.

Sometimes it took a few days, sometimes a couple of weeks. When the flower finally died, I would take it outside, say good-bye to it, and thank it for giving its life for me and for delivering my prayer. Then I would bury it so it would have a chance at a new life, and I always hoped it would come back as an even nicer flower.

In this simple, graphic way my mother taught me how uplifting prayer can be. And, in the process, she taught me about life, too – how basic both dying and rising are to living and how important it is that we become Sacrifice Flowers for each other.

The Spelling Test

8

When I was in the second grade I had an experience that determined what I was going to do with my life.

My teacher was Miss James. She had 80 of us in her class – if you can imagine that! She was older and unmarried, but she had the power to bring life out of people. And that's exactly what she did for me when I was caught in a situation in which it looked as if I had cheated.

I was in pretty heavy competition with a boy in my class, George. He was better in arithmetic, I was better in spelling. I was better in reading, he was better in science. The teacher encouraged this competition between the two of us, and among the other kids as well; in fact, she seemed to have contests going all the time. There were so many that, eventually, every kid won something. On this particular occasion, we were having a contest between the girls and the boys. George had won for the boys in arithmetic, putting them one ahead, and there was one contest left – spelling – and the girls were sort of counting on me, because that was one of my best subjects.

The spelling test had 20 words. I took my spelling book out and carefully reviewed the words. We took the test and passed in our papers, and they were graded. George missed one and I got a perfect paper.

While Miss James was telling us about the results, a little guy who sat kitty-corner from me looked over at me and saw that my spelling book was still out on top of my desk. And he said, "She should have got 100. She cheated. There's the book out on top of her desk." I hadn't looked at the book. I hadn't even noticed it was out on top of my desk instead of inside where it should have been while we were taking the test. But the evidence was against me, and clearly it said, "The book is out and she cheated."

I felt horrible. Now we were going to lose. I sat there. Tears welled up in my eyes. I was scared. I was hurt. I was disappointed. Miss James came back and stood by my desk. I couldn't look up at her. I knew that if I did I would start saying I was guilty, and I wasn't. Then she said to me, "Jo, did you look at that book?" I was so broken up that I couldn't even talk, so I shook my head no. And she said, "Well now, don't worry about it. I believe you." She believed me! I could hardly believe myself, because that spelling book on the corner of my desk looked so incriminating.

The bell rang. Class was over. I just sat there. I couldn't get over it. It was as if she had saved my life. One second I felt like I was drowning; the next she was pulling me back in, saving my reputation and doing in the kid who had falsely accused me. A lot of good things happened to me right there. I sat in the back of the room for a long time. I thought, "That's what I am going to be when I grow up. I'm going to be what she is. I am going to do for kids what she just did for me."

The next day I asked my dad for money to buy a notebook. From that time on, I used it to keep track of things that my teachers did – what I liked and what I did not like, what the other kids liked and what they did not like. It became my way of trying to become as good a teacher as I could. And I did become a teacher, first in the classroom and then beyond the classroom.

What Miss James did for me still lives on in my life. She taught me to trust, to care, to support. She helped me to understand Christ as teacher. And she is a model for the kind of teachers we could all be for each other.

The Hugging Prayer

9

My mother taught me many prayers when I was young. Often they were prayers of comfort, in contrast to those of my father. His prayers taught me to meet life's challenges.

I did not always think of my mother's prayers as prayers, even though that's what she called them. Sometimes I just went through them with her to satisfy her. Nevertheless, because they were based on experience, many of them stuck with me.

This is one of my favorites. I was about six years old at the time I learned this one. I was sitting outside on a block of concrete, and I was crying. I don't even know why. I was just crying and crying. My mother came along and said, "What's the matter?" I said, "Nothing. Leave me alone!" She did – and then I really started crying. About 15 minutes later she came back and sat beside me. "You know," she said, "I have to tell you something. There are going to be a lot of times in your life when you are going to cry, and you won't know why. You won't understand and neither will anybody else. You can marry the nicest man in the world, but at times like this, he won't know what to do to help you stop crying."

Then she said she was going to teach me a prayer for the times when I was crying and didn't know why. She made me get off the cement block and stand up. She said, "Now put your arms around yourself." I did, but it wasn't good enough for her. "You're just folding your arms," she said. "Put them all the way around yourself. Cuddle your body. Hold yourself the way you would hold a baby in your arms."

"Now after you have a real good hold of yourself, close your eyes and begin to rock yourself. Rock yourself real good, the way you would a baby, and just keep doing it. When you grow up, no matter how old you are, and you find yourself crying and you don't know why, I want you to rock yourself just like this. And as you do it, remember that you are God's little girl, and that God understands why you are crying even if no one else does. And remember, too, that God holds you close just the way you are holding yourself, because God loves you very much. Then just keep rocking yourself and be comforted."

Isn't that a good prayer? I still say it today when I feel bad. I recommend it for you, too. Just stand wherever you are – in the kitchen, in the shop, or in the bathroom – and wrap your arms around yourself as tightly as you can. Rock yourself.

Before long you will be able to feel God holding you in the same way you are holding yourself. You will be comforted the way you were comforted as a child when your mother held you in her arms and rocked you.

The Medicine Bag

10

When children were born in my family, they got a special birth gift. My father made us each a little leather pouch – our own little medicine bag. It was something he learned from my mother, who was a Seneca Iroquois.

My mother put two things in it, and so did my dad. Then they gave the medicine bag to us, and we were to put it in a special place. If you died without your medicine bag, as some of my brothers did during the war, then it was buried separately. Otherwise the medicine bag was buried with you. When we got old enough to understand, we were told what was in our medicine bag. One thing my mother put in mine was a pinch of land from the state of Texas. That's because I was born there. Imagine – putting Texas in a bag! She also kept a piece of umbilical cord from my birth, about two inches. She dried it in the sun. Then she put this into the bag, crumbling it into the Texas soil. These two things, the cord and the pinch of Texas, symbolized that I came out of the land and out of my parents. They were to help me remember that I didn't start out by myself, that I was dependent upon the land and upon my family.

My father put a bird feather into each child's medicine bag. He burned a small part of the feather and mixed it in with the things mother had put in. The reason was that birds were of the sky. They can soar to the horizon and beyond. The feather said that each of us was to soar, also, and find our own place in the world.

None of us ever knew what other item dad put into our bags. It represented the unknown, the mystery in life. No matter how we tried, he would not tell us. We had our suspicions and we guessed and guessed, but he would never even give us a hint.

To have a mystery set before me like this early in life proved a big help when I began to work with the mysteries in my life that came along later. It also helped me to understand that God is the center of all mystery.

I still have my medicine bag. It was a wonderful gift from my parents, and it has shown me the importance of making symbols that tie us to places and to people and to God.

My Favorite Day

11

When I was growing up, my favorite day of the week was Tuesday. Tuesday was ironing day. From the time I was a very little girl, my mother and I did the ironing on Tuesday. Once I got into school, we did it after I got home. For the first few years, my iron wasn't hot. I had a little toy one. Then I got a real iron and began to work on simple things like handkerchiefs and napkins. Slowly I moved up to pillowcases and shirts, and finally to large tablecloths that took a very long time.

I loved Tuesdays, not only because I was doing just what my mother did and she was teaching me to do it well, but also because it was the time when I met my mother in her girlhood. We would often just waste time together. The men in the family were on their own that day.

Sometimes we got out the photo album and looked at pictures from my mother's youth. We put it on the desk near our workplace and looked at the photos and talked about them. We were sharing our lives. I would tell her about my comings and goings, how I was doing in school, what I thought about things. My mother would tell me about herself and she would sing the songs she learned as a young girl and teach them to me. I, too, would teach her the songs I had learned in school or heard on the radio.

My mother showed me pictures of her boyfriends, and I would wonder about her life. And Tuesdays were the days when I got my sex education. My mother talked about everything. It was an ideal place for her to do it; she didn't have to be constantly looking at me. She asked me one question over and over again. What do you think are the most important things to look for in the man you are going to marry? My answer to her question usually centered on the usual things – handsome, red convertible, lots of money – things that are important when you're in the fourth grade. The requirements would change from year to year. In the seventh grade my man had to be good at basketball. In the eighth grade, he had to like poetry.

One Tuesday it occurred to me to ask my mother what she had looked for when she got married. I can't remember all of her requirements, but two of them stick in my mind. One was that he had to have a good sense of humor. She also would say that spirituality was very important to her. He had to be a person with some sense of the meaning of life and of what was really important. When she told me that, it changed the way I looked at my mother and father. I began to see love in a more adult way. I began to see how choices can make a real difference in one's life.

12

The Sensuous Bedroom

A few years ago while flying from Chicago to Tampa to give a retreat on Native American spirituality, I became very tired, too tired for writing letters or working on talks, and so I decided I would relax for a couple of hours with the flight magazine.

But when I pulled the flight magazine from the back of the seat in front of me, it wasn't what I expected. It was a magazine somebody had left behind. Okay, I thought, I will just go with that. To tell you the truth, I was looking for something to put me to sleep and I thought this magazine would do it as well as anything. I flipped through the pages and came upon a review of a book titled *The Sensuous Bedroom*. I thought, now that looks like a good subject for a nun! After all, I can't limit myself to reading just religious titles, because most of life doesn't have religious titles. Think of how much humanity I would miss.

I started reading. Right away I was struck by how well-written and well-organized this book review was. For example, the reviewer pointed out that the book's author said there are six characteristics of a sensuous bedroom, and he went on to describe each one. As I finished, I thought, "Wow, what a parallel for prayer life!" I could also see it was something I might be able to use someday, and so I filed it away in my mind.

The occasion came sooner than I expected. When I got to Tampa, the sister in charge of the retreat center, who met me at the airport, said, "Sister, we don't want to impose on you, but we have a staff of 50 volunteers who help us. Some of them have heard your tapes and they said they would like to hear you in person. Could you give them a talk tonight? You could talk on anything you want."

"On anything?" I said.

"On anything," she said.

"Sure," I said, "I'll give a talk, and without hesitating I told her my topic would be "The Sensuous Bedroom and Your Prayer Life." I could tell by the look on her face that she was shocked. We sat in silence as she drove in the rest of the way from the airport.

By the time we got to the retreat center, she had recovered a bit. In the dining room, she got everyone's attention and said I had graciously agreed to give a talk and she even managed to get out the title. Just as she did, someone dropped a fork –otherwise it was perfectly still. As I started thinking about what I was going to say –by that time there were only two hours before my talk – I noticed people were springing into action. There were phone calls, cars going and coming, quiet and polite inquiries.

To my surprise, we had a huge crowd. I was out talking to some of the people who came, including two newly married couples. One of the husbands asked me if I were really going to talk on the topic he had been informed about. "You bet," I said, "and it's going to be good. You better take notes." Later, I noticed that he did take notes.

Here then are the six characteristics of a sensuous bedroom and their parallels to prayer.

First. "Put the bed in the middle of the room." This signifies that whatever you do in bed, including your dreaming and lovemaking, is important. With the bed in the center of the room, you can't ignore it. You bump into it, stumble over it, or walk around it.

Give prayer the same place in your life. Put it at the center, and you'll soon find the Holy Spirit is at the center of your life too. Then you will really have something to bump into or try to get around.

Second, to have a really sensuous bedroom, you have to "elevate the bed" – putting it up on casters or a platform. This signifies your time alone, or your time of intimacy, is to be elevated. What you do in bed is not base and coarse, but beautiful and high.

What is your prayer about if it is not about elevating? In prayer, we are taking the ordinary stuff of everyday life and lifting it up, elevating it so we are taken to a higher level of thought, of delight, of passion for living, of action.

Third, a sensuous bedroom needs things in it that are "soft and curvaceous." There should be something circular rather than having everything at sharp angles. This is obvious because lovemaking is all about going in circles – embracing, caressing, enfolding, holding. And isn't that just what prayer is about? Prayer helps us to deal with what is sharp and angular. It helps us to allow ourselves to be embraced, caressed, and made love to by God, and to return God's love by caressing and embracing, and making love to the people in our lives.

Fourth, according to the review, a sensuous bedroom has to have a couple of bronzed mirrors. Why bronzed? Because, as the author of the review explains, people can't always take the image of their own reality. Too many people are too shy to have mirrors reflect their bodies back to them. So they need the bronze to soften the image in order to deal with their nakedness.

We find the same thing is true with prayer. Prayer is concerned with reflection – reflecting on the word, reflecting on God's love for us, and reflecting on how we are to love the people around us. Without such reflection, the realities of life would be very harsh. Further, we are asked to reflect God's love to those around us. Without prayer, that would not only be difficult but impossible.

I am crazy about the last two characteristics of the sensuous bedroom. I just love them. They are the wild ones. The first is to get rid of the bedspread! Why? So that when you have a spontaneous moment of passion or desire, you can act on it. You don't have to fold up the spread first. You are free to allow yourself to give and to be taken.

What does that have to do with prayer? One reason we don't pray more is that we always have to have the props of formality in front of us – our prayerbooks, for example – so we get the wording just right. But the props, like the bedspread, can get in the way of spontaneous response to God. When you pray, say what is in your heart, laughing or crying or yearning yourself toward God.

Finally, a sensuous bedroom must have a symbol of an appetite other than the sexual. Its purpose is to remind us that love is not just a sexual experience, but a total experience, one involving the whole person. A bowl of fruit would be a good example. Or a bottle of wine and a couple of glasses. Or a beautiful painting.

This characteristic certainly relates to prayer. Prayer, too, is a total experience. For example, we decorate altars. We have vestments. We use music. All of these are symbols showing our relationship to God is holistic and doesn't concern only just one part of our being.

Aren't these six characteristics of a sensuous bedroom wonderful images of prayer?

After the retreat, I went to Dallas to give some talks. A priest met me at the airport. As we talked in the car, he suddenly said, "José, wait until you see the bedroom where you'll be sleeping tonight!" Not quite sure what to say, I finally asked, "Where am I staying?" "In the rectory guest room," he replied, adding, "The pastor told me not to do what I did, because he said you wouldn't think it was funny, but I thought you'd love it, so I went ahead." When I tried to get him to tell me more, he would not. "You'll see," he said.

When we got to the rectory, we went up to the guest room and he opened the door. There I saw a plain single bed with a table, desk, chair and lamp. "I don't see anything unusual about this," I said. "Take off the bedspread," he answered. I did. The sheets had a leopard skin design. "Wow," I said. "This is going to bring out the animal in me, but there's one thing missing."

"What's that?" he asked.

"A bowl of fruit."

He went to get one. My stay there was filled with sensuous prayer.

13 The Sleeping Ute

One of the most important lessons my mother taught me as a child was how we must learn to let the land around us live in our hearts and in our memories.

I grew up in the southwest near Mesa Verde country. Right out our kitchen window you could see the great mountain formation called the Sleeping Ute. In fact, the sun went down every night right into the arms of this enormous Indian figure. This magnificent arrangement of mountains lies spread across southwestern Colorado for about 14 miles. You can plainly see in the outlines of the mountain a war bonnet, the silhouette of a body with arms folded across his chest and moccasins on his feet.

There is a Native American legend that goes with the Sleeping Ute, of course. He was a great leader of his people in the past who become overwhelmed, overcome in a tremendous battle against the Evil Ones. This great warrior was wounded in the struggle, so he lay down to rest and fell into a deep sleep. He rests on the land, but someday he will rise up and lead his people once again. When fog or clouds settle over the sleeping warrior, it is a sign that he is changing his blankets. When the native people saw the light green blanket over their warrior hero, they knew then that it was spring. The dark green blanket was summer, the yellow and red one was autumn, and the white blanket was winter. When clouds gathered on the highest peaks, it was a sign that the great warrior was pleased with his people and was letting rain clouds slip from his pockets. Even today Sleeping Ute Mountain in used by the people who live nearby to forecast the weather.

When the sun would start to go down over the Sleeping Ute, my mother would come to me and say, "Come out here and spend some time looking at the land. Memorize it. Someday you will live where there are no mountains, where you don't have this beautiful land you have here. So look at the land, spend some time with it, study it, and learn it until you understand something about it. Take it into your heart."

"You are a little girl now and you can't foresee this, but one day you will get lonely for your land. Someday you will find that your heart is yearning for a chance to see this land again. Then you won't want your memory of it to be sketchy and blurry. You will want it clear in your mind and heart. You will want to be able to see the colors and the way the shadows fall at different times of day."

I did not completely understand then what she was saying, but I did remember the land. Also, when we walked along a dusty country road, my mother would say, "Feel the earth. Your feet are trying to teach you about the land. Someday your toes will not be walking in this warm dirt, but your feet will remember the road, and this will make you happy."

My mother said that people who are not homesick for the land, the weeds, the grass and flowers and trees that helped them grow up, probably would not hurt too much either from homesickness for those they love. As I have grown older, I have found myself fingering the memories of such moments and scenes. My mother helped me create a string of beauty for remembering.

It was very Native American in tradition. And I think it is something we need to do as American people, as a people living on this continent. It might be just the remedy we need to stop destroying so much of our beautiful country. We must take the land into our hearts and love it.

Spilled Milk

14

We carry scars from our childhood. They heal over and sometimes they hardly show but they are there and can be raised in our memories, especially when similar things happen to us. I have one such scar dating back to the time I was eight years old. In the southwest where I grew up, certain places did not serve Native Americans. Some put up signs saying, "No Indians Served." Others were more subtle; they didn't serve Indians but didn't put up signs either. They had other little ways of getting the message across.

One day my mother – who was a beautiful full-blood Indian with lovely, long black hair – and I were shopping. We decided to take a break and get something to drink. We sat down in a booth, with a formica tabletop and nice green leather seats. I will never forget that booth. I will always remember the name of the restaurant, too, though I won't mention it here. Mom sat on one side of the booth, I on the other. She ordered a cup of coffee. I got a glass of milk.

The waitress brought my milk, but she didn't bring my mother's coffee. Instead she went over to the cash register and stood. I walked over to her and said, "You forgot my mother's coffee." She just looked at me, didn't say anything, but didn't bring the coffee either.

We waited a bit. Then my mother said, "Jo, I think this is one of those places that won't serve Indian people. I don't think she's going to bring my cup of coffee." I remember sitting there looking at my mother, thinking how beautiful she was and wondering how anyone could do this. I was more than half Indian myself, though I didn't look it because I was fairer and had brown hair. And because of that, I got served and my mother did not. I got very angry. Furious, would be more accurate.

My mother said she thought we should go. We got up. As we did, I took my glass of milk – in those days when you ordered a glass of milk you got a real glass and a big glass – and slowly poured it over the back of both sides of the booth, across the seats, over the tabletop, and all over the floor. I did as much damage with one glass of milk as I could. Then I picked up the water glasses and did the same thing with them.

By the time I had finished, there was a real mess. If they weren't going to serve my mother, I remember thinking, then they were going to remember they didn't serve her. I was going to give them a cleanup job they wouldn't forget.

My mother didn't say anything. She didn't correct me. She didn't stop me. She just stood a little distance away and watched. When I had emptied all the glasses and made as big a mess as I could, she said, "Well now, Jo, you have proven yourself to be just as stupid as they are."

That stumped me at the time. But in thinking about it later, I realized she had taught me a lesson. I knew I was angry and knew I had a right to be. But my mother's response taught me this: Even when you might feel you are justified, don't respond in kind when violence has been done to you. She was saying there are other ways to respond. It isn't always an eye for an eye, a tooth for a tooth. Vengeance is not the way.

Since then I have experienced discrimination many times – as a Native American, as a woman, as a woman in the church. I have tried, on each occasion, to remember my mother's lesson. She was calling me to a different kind of response, a peaceful and nonviolent one. It is a response, by the way, that is at the heart of the life and teaching of Jesus.

That doesn't mean you don't fight for what you believe in. It doesn't mean you stand back and let people walk all over you. But to take on the tactics of ignorance, discrimination and prejudice poisons you, sours your heart, and embitters your life.

We have had many wonderful spiritual leaders in the Native American traditions. Their message has always been the same: Even though you have experienced injustice, even though your

34

land has been taken away and your way of life destroyed, even though there have been efforts to actually wipe you out as a people, do not let your heart become sour and respond in kind, for if you do, those who made you turn sour will win in the end.

My mother passed that message on to me that day. Spilled milk can do nothing but turn sour. An angry, vengeful heart will too. Keep your heart sweet, she was saying, the way milk in a glass is.

A Thanksgiving Guest

My mother loved older people. When I was a child, she used to send my brothers and me off with gifts for them – a plate of cookies, freshly baked bread, Easter eggs in baskets. She always looked after older people.

One day she sent me to visit an elderly lady name Mrs. Casey. It was a very difficult mission for a child because Mrs. Casey had cancer and, as a result, she had no nose. Her face was flat and bandaged from her eyes to her mouth. Her disease also caused a bad smell. Visiting Mrs. Casey was an ordeal, particularly since my mother expected me to sit and talk.

After a couple of visits, I told my mother to have one of my brothers visit Mrs. Casey. I didn't want to see her again. That was all my mother needed to make sure I kept on going to see Mrs. Casey. I dreaded it every time, but I always sat and visited, like my mother wanted.

One day, in November, my mother announced she had invited Mr. and Mrs. Casey over for Thanksgiving dinner. I objected, saying the smell would ruin my dinner. My mother told me I would to have to adjust because the Caseys didn't have anyplace to go. I thought about the baked turkey and the pumpkin pies and my all-time Thanksgiving favorite –sweet potatoes. Not wanting to miss any of it, I told my mother I would sit at the opposite end of the table.

But on Thanksgiving my mother sat me directly across from Mrs. Casey. I kept my eyes down and tried to be polite. But keeping my eyes down proved difficult, especially when the sweet potatoes started coming around. They were filled with marshmallows and brown sugar – just the way I liked them. But as the sweet potatoes came to my brother, he took two. That was against a house rule we had, saying you took only one of anything until everyone had been served. But my brother thought he was clever. He could see I was the last one to be served and wouldn't get any if he took two. He also knew that with the company present I couldn't object, as I surely would have otherwise.

When the sweet potato platter got to Mrs. Casey, she counted the number of people and saw that I wouldn't get any, so she passed it on without taking one. When it got to me there was still one left. *I felt terrible!* I took it, and I'm glad to say I had the good grace to cut it in half and offer a portion to Mrs. Casey. When I did, a strange thing happened. She didn't smell anymore. She looked like a lovely person. She smiled back at me, took the potato, and we had a great Thanksgiving dinner.

Later, when I learned about the life of St. Francis, I came to see this Thanksgiving encounter as similar to the conversion experience he had when he embraced the leper. I learned never to let a scar on a person's outside, no matter how ugly, keep me from seeing the beauty on the inside.

A Moment to Remember

16

Memory is wonderful. I like remembering. I have come to think of it as a way of recycling experiences. Sometimes I have more fun with an old memory than with a new experience. When I tell people that they almost always say it's because I'm getting old. I disagree.

One of my favorite memories – a funny one – is of something that happened at the Stapleton Airport in Denver. I still think about it, even though it took place 15 years ago, and, as often as not, I have a good laugh in remembering it.

For years I have been speaking around the country, traveling great distances. As a result, I have gotten acquainted with the ins and outs of many airports, and I have learned to take plenty of work with me for long lay-overs. When I have such a stop, I seek out a quiet place, open my bag and get to work on my mail and speaking dates.

The Denver airport had a great spot for this. It was on the lower level, at the far end of the luggage carousels.

It had a large desk and a comfortable office chair, with a post office nearby. It had everything I needed, and I never failed to get a lot of work done there. For someone on the move, this was a wonderful place to land.

One day while working there, I noticed two men sitting across from me. They were very different from each other – so different that I wondered why they were together. They didn't speak. The younger man seemed pleasant and relaxed. He wore slacks and a sport shirt. The other, dressed in a suit and looking like a businessman, seemed quite stern. He didn't smile and paid no attention to anyone, including the younger man next to him. He struck me as rather dour.

After working nearly two hours, I needed a break. A little walk would do me good, I decided. I travel light and take only one's bag. It contains all my papers and my clothes. I could not chance leaving it unattended, but I did not want to rent a locker for such a short time. I decided to do what I usually did in such cases. I would ask someone who looked honest to watch my bag.

I sized up the two men. Which one to ask? The dour-faced man might be more responsible, but he also looked as if he might say no. I went for the pleasant one. He seemed more my type. He responded as I expected, saying with a smile, "Oh yes, lady, I'd be glad to." The other man seemed startled by what I had asked, but said nothing and looked at me in a way that made me doubly glad I hadn't asked him.

I walked for 15 minutes. I thanked the young man and went back to work. Less than a half hour later, a uniformed policeman, clearly on official business, approached the two men and spoke to the businessman. As he did, the two men got up and I saw they were handcuffed together! Immediately, it became clear which one was in custody – it was the one I'd ask to watch my bag.

As they got ready to leave, my curiosity got the best of me. I went over to the young man and asked, "What are they taking you in for?" Giving me the most pleasant grin I think I have ever seen, he answered, "Breaking and entering, lady!" I smiled back and both of us started laughing. Imagine, asking a burglar to guard your possessions! The uniformed policeman, knowing nothing of what had gone on, stood straight-faced. The other man didn't see anything funny, but the two of us did. Of all the people going though the airport that day, I picked him! The more we laughed, the funnier it got.

I always smile when I remember it – and often I even laugh again. I never knew the young man's name, but I often think of him and the moment we shared. It was something to remember. And I do recall it with pleasure – not because I am getting old, but because it keeps me young.

On the Way to Ajo

17

When I lived in Tucson in the late 1970s, I had an experience that helped me to see how we can make scripture come alive in our lives. I had heard and read how we were to relate our experience and our life's story to the scriptural story, and I'm sure I had done it before, but this experience made it clear in a way that words couldn't.

Raymond, a 12-year-old neighbor boy, and I had become friends. He was the leader of kids in the neighborhood, which was poor and crowded. He was handsome (half Apache and half Hispanic), vital, mischievous, and rather spiritual (although he would never let his buddies know that).

One Sunday afternoon, as I was reading scripture, he knocked on my door. "What are you doing, Sis?" I told him I was reading a parable, explaining that a parable was a story Jesus told to wake us up to life. "Why don't you read it to me?" he said. The parable was the Good Samaritan. I didn't think a story about an incident on the road from Jerusalem to Jericho would mean much to him, so I decided to relocate the story in telling it to him.

The road from Tucson to Ajo, 125 miles to the west, is desolate and hot. It's such a tough stretch that even a young boy would know about it, making it the perfect location for this story. "It was kind of like this, Raymond," I started. "This guy was on the road from Tucson to Ajo. It was hot, about 115 degrees. He had an old pickup that coughed along, and he came to a man standing by the road. He stopped to give the man a ride and, as he did, the man grabbed him, beat him, threw him in the ditch, took his canteen and drove off in his car."

Raymond interrupted, "Boy, that was a lousy thing to do, especially taking the man's the water." I agreed. We talked about the desolate road and that not many people pass by, especially during such heat. "Eventually," I went on, "a man did pass by, a salesman, but he was in a hurry to see his next customer and kept right on going." I could see Raymond didn't approve.

"Soon another man, a young fellow in a nice car, came by. He saw the injured man but he was afraid and said to himself, 'You just never know what you might pick up these days – I better not risk it.' And so he drove on, too." By now Raymond was irritated, because even though only a boy he knew you did not pass by people on this stretch of road on such a hot day.

I went on: "Pretty soon a priest, on his way to a mission to say mass, come down the road." Raymond chimed in, "Well, he_didn't pass him up." "Well, yes, Raymond, he did," I said. "He had to get to the church on time and thought he'd have somebody go back to help." By now, Raymond was disgusted, and I knew I had to bring the next character along without delay!

So I interrupted Raymond: "In the distance a small figure appeared – a man walking. It took a long time before you could see what the man looked like. He was a hippie –his hair was long, he was dusty, and he probably had everything he owned in his backpack. When he saw the man by the roadside, he took his canteen, gave him a drink and washed his face. Then he hitched a ride into Ajo for both of them. He took the man to a clinic, told what had happened, and got in touch with the man's family so they could take him home."

When I finished, I asked the question Jesus asked: "Which of these men, Raymond, would you want as your neighbor?" "Boy, I want the guy who stopped and helped," Raymond said. For a while after that, we talked about the story and how some people help others and some don't. But then his friends came along and he had to go out and play.

A few months later, Raymond came banging on my screen door. I had never seen him so excited. "Sis! Sis!" he yelled, "I went to church today. Guess what! We had a story almost *exactly* like that guy on the way from Tucson to Ajo." I'd never seen anyone so excited about hearing a gospel story. The reason: He had made a connection between something that happened in his life and the scripture.

His excitement helped me to realize in a special way that that is what we are to do with scripture – make connections between it and our lives. Raymond did and he felt excitement. I do when I make the connection, and I'm sure you will, too.

Flunking Kindergarten

18

After a few days in kindergarten, I didn't like it. It was too boring. I had done most of the things we were supposed to do. They taught us how to tie our shoes, and I had been tying mine a couple of years. They made me lie down and rest when I wasn't tired. They made me drink lukewarm milk and eat crackers when I wasn't hungry and didn't like lukewarm milk. They made me draw pictures inside lines when I wanted to be creative.

After a couple of weeks, I found excitement. During recess, I met a nice policeman, Officer Bob. He had parked at the curb on a motorcycle, with a sidecar. He asked if I would like a ride. I asked the teacher's permission. I could see she did not like the idea, but she did not want to tell the policemen no, so she said I could.

Officer Bob told me all about the motorcycle, a Harley-Davidson, and what it could do. He even revved it up for me. I loved the ride. Apparently Officer Bob did too, because he came back to give me more rides. Soon, we had three or four kids in the sidecar. The rides became the highlight of my day. In addition to enjoying them, they became a kind of victory over my teacher. I was doing what she did not really want me to do. Further, they got me away from my boring kindergarten.

But Officer Bob didn't come every day. On those days, I played on the fire escape. It was one of those covered ones that wrap around the building like a worm. I spent recess climbing up and sliding down that fire escape.

At the end of the year, we got a report card. I gave mine to my mother. She responded with shock because it said I failed. The teacher explained I did only two things well – and you can imagine what they were. "I don't care if I failed," I told my mother.

"It was so dull. I'm just glad to get out of there." But my mother took a different approach. "Jo," she said, "I don't like this. I don't think you did what you should have. You're going to have to learn you can't run away from a situation you don't like or that doesn't interest you. If a thing bores for you, it's boring because you're boring. When things are boring, try to make them exciting. Be creative."

I could not believe what she said next. She said I would have to repeat kindergarten. That shot my summer, I can tell you that. But my mother held firm and that fall, back I went. She took me to school. After she and the teacher talked, my mother told me I would have to stay in kindergarten until the teacher said I could go on to the first grade.

This time, I cooperated. I went into action. I jumped into everything, because I wanted to get out of there. I made kids drink their milk. I slept at nap time. I made sure everyone else did, too – which, by the way, was not easy!

After two weeks, the teacher decided I could go into first grade. Sometimes, I think I drove her crazy and she wanted to get rid of me. In any event, I moved on without regrets. I laugh about it now – I mean, how many people do you know who flunked kindergarten?! I remember pain, too. But I learned from the experience. Never again did I let myself get bored. When I got into a boring situation, I got busy – thinking, imagining, doing whatever I could to create. Once I had a very boring job as an inventory clerk for International Harvester. I made it interesting for myself. I learned all I could from the people around me, including the salesman. I learned the names of the machine parts and how they worked. Before I finished I not only to liked what I did but I learned to appreciate something entirely new.

With my mother's help, flunking kindergarten taught me that I am responsible for keeping life from being boring. Over the years, in trying to make boring situations exciting, I developed confidence in my own creativity. I also found that grace hides everywhere, and that we work out our salvation in ordinary situations which, at first glance, may seem boring.

How Old Is 40?

19

When I worked on the Fort Peck Indian Reservation, in northeastern Montana, I lived next door to a family with a little girl named Patrice, a non-stop bundle of energy. On Saturday mornings she came over to my house. She would do Native American dances for me one minute, read to me the next. When I cooked, she climbed up on a stool next to me, as close as she could get. She even did it when I washed dishes.

One Saturday, she asked, "Sister, how old are you?" I said, "I'm 40. How old are you?" "I'm six," she said. She didn't say anything for a minute. I could see her thinking, and I sensed her next question would be a big one. She didn't disappoint me: "Just how old is 40, anyway?" I didn't know what to say. I had never thought about it. She had stumped me. But then, in desperation – or perhaps inspiration – I got an idea.

I told Patrice I would take her for a walk and sent her to ask her mother. I knew her mother would be thrilled to have someone looking after this bundle of energy for a few hours. Patrice and I headed for a road going out into the Montana countryside. "Now, I'm going to teach you how old 40 is," I said to her, "and here at the start you're going to be four years old, okay?" She agreed.

The first stretch goes uphill. We soon came to a dump. It smelled and smoked. I made that our first landmark. "Okay Patrice," I said, "at this dump, you're six years old." I also made another connection between her and the dump. "In some ways, kids are a like dumps. They have little things burning inside them, the way dumps do. These are things they have to deal with."

We came to a decline. As we started down, we came across wild rose bushes along the edge of the road. I talked about the thorns and how they can hurt you. By now she got the hang of this. After I finished, she asked, "Okay, how old am I now?" "Ten." Near the bottom of the decline, she fell, and I said, "Now you're 16." When the road started up again, she said, "Sister, I'm tired, could you carry me." "Now, Patrice," I answered, "I can't carry a 16-year-old girl!"

When we got all the way to the top of the first hill – about half a mile from where we started – I said, "You've come a long way, now you're 20." "Oh, Sister," she said, "I'm getting so tired, won't I be 40 pretty soon? I hope we don't have very far to go." I could see she couldn't take much more so I said, "When we get to the top of this next hill, you'll be 40."

We started again. Now she slowed even more. I not only held her hand but carried her some. We came to ruts in the road. I stumbled and both of us nearly fell. "That was 30," I said. We began the final ascent. When we got to the top I seated her on a big rock. We looked out at a beautiful scene, with the Missouri River below and hills in the distance. "Now, Patrice, you're 40," I said triumphantly. "Maybe now you can tell me how old 40 is."

She looked around and brightened up. Finally, she said, "You can see a lot farther when you are 40 – and it's really pretty – but you're sure a lot more tired." I laughed all the way back to town, even though I did have to carry her the last quarter mile or so.

I recall this little episode each year on my birthday, and I say a prayer for Patrice (who, as I write, is 26). Each birthday, as I review our little walk, I ask myself, how old am I now? How tired am I now? How far have I come? How much farther do I have to go? How was my walk this past year? How much of it was uphill? Where were the dumps? How many thorns did I encounter? How many declines did I have? Did I walk hand-in-hand with others? Did I carry anyone? How many carried me? Did we catch each other when we stumbled? Can I see farther than the year before?

I took Patrice for the walk in a playful way to teach her about growing up and getting older, but it led to an annual reflection that helps me to focus on the big questions in my journey through life.

46

Don't Be a Deadhead

20

I first heard the word deadhead at the Denver Museum of National History. I had stopped to admire a beautiful rose garden out front. I noticed one tall rose with a large bud that drooped over. I asked a man doing pruning why a rose would do that. "It's a deadhead," he said. He explained deadhead, as a botanical term, referred to roses that have strong stems and full buds but collapse instead of blooming.

The notion of deadhead intrigued me. I decided to do some research. I found the word deadhead also refers to a railroad boxcar that comes back empty after taking a load to a destination. I started to think of a deadhead as anything that doesn't fulfill its potential, that doesn't live up to its promise.

I began applying this notion to people, including myself. Why did I go deadhead at certain points or places in my life? Why did deadhead seem such an accurate metaphor for many people's lives? Was it fear of opening up? Of blooming? False pride that blossoming would be misunderstood as arrogance or pride? Or, was it the knowledge, perhaps unconscious, that after blooming comes death? With these questions fresh in my mind, I stopped at the book store at the Denver airport to get a mystery – it's my favorite escape literature – to read on my way to a speaking engagement. I couldn't have come across a more perfect book: *Deadheads* (yes, it had a big rose on the cover) by Reginald Hill, a British mystery writer and one of my favorites. This was almost too much – a favorite writer on my topic of the moment.

The book, based on an actual case, tells the story of a man abandoned as a child. He lived with his grandmother, who raised roses. When he reached age 14, she mysteriously disappeared. As the only heir, he got her property, including, of course, all the roses. Later, he married a woman who liked roses and she, too, disappeared without explanation. Over a 20-year period, so did four or five other people, all with connections to this man and to roses.

Reginald Hill never quite pins the murders on the man, but he proposes the theory that he turned into a deadhead. Somehow or other he had come to a crucial point in his life, or in his relationship with people, and he could not continue, could not deliver. The tragedies followed.

In telling me about deadheads, the man at the Denver Museum had said, "I think some roses never burst forth because in their stems there's a memory of storms and winds that will blow them apart if they open up and so they would rather die on the vine, literally, rather than take the risk of being exposed to life."

I suspect this happened to the man in the mystery. I suspect it happens to many of us, too. We allow memories and fears to keep us from fulfilling our potential. We find it easier, safer, not to risk blossoming. For example, as a teacher of prayer, I run into many people who fear contemplative prayer. They pray – often more than I do –but they stick with rote or communal prayer, and never really get into the realm of mystery.

It's sad to see a rose droop and fail to flower. It's even sadder to see people do it. When we do, I think we not only fail to reach our potential, we also reject God who is present in our lives, working to help us realize our potential. Accept yourself, accept God. Don't be a deadhead.

Wiping Away Burdens

21

Like most people, I have trouble getting rid of burdens from the past, with the result that I carry around excess baggage. I would have even more except for a Native American ritual I learned years ago.

Native Americans call it "Wiping Away the Burdens." It comes from the Crow and Northern Cheyenne tribes. I first learned it when I went to a reservation to help teach Indian children. Tribal leaders used at the start of the school to wipe away negative memories of the past year so they would not interfere with the year ahead.

I asked tribal leaders if I could share the ritual with others. They said yes. Since then, I have found it an effective ritual, especially when beginning something new or making a new start on something old. In addition to a new school year, New Year's Day becomes an obvious time for it. So does the beginning of a liturgical year.

The ritual unfolds this way: One person, often an elder, fasts in preparation, usually for a day. When the ritual begins, that person stands by as a symbol of power. Another person wipes away burdens by using a cloth fastened to a stick. The cloth should be brightly colored and about an inch wide and a yard long. The stick should also be about a yard in length. One at a time, the persons participating step forward and sit in a chair or kneel. The person wiping away the burdens takes a position behind each one who comes forward. Holding the stick, the person doing the wiping drags or draws the cloth over each person five times, twice over each shoulder and once over the head. First, to wipe away the past, the wiper draws the cloth across each shoulder from back to front. Second, to wipe away anxieties about the future, the wiper draws the cloth across each shoulder from front to back. Finally, to wipe away unpleasant memories, the wiper draws the cloth over the head, from back to front. A key moment in the ceremony follows. After the cloth has been drawn over the person's head, the wiper holds it in front of the individual for a moment so all can focus on it. Then the wiper gives it a snap, or a flick, and, at the same time, everyone, including the person who has stepped forward, joins in a collective but silent, "Let it go." Traditionally, the ritual concludes in silence, without music or audible prayers. This follows the Native American custom of relying on action rather than words in rituals.

In addition to performing the ritual by itself, I have used it in conjunction with the sacrament of reconciliation. In doing that, I usually begin with a scripture reading. I follow that with the wiping away ritual and conclude with the celebration of the communal form of the sacrament of reconciliation.

When I have a large group, we gather in one place for the scripture reading. The wiping away ritual, however, works best with 15 to 20 people, so I break the participants into small groups for that. After the ritual, I bring the small groups back together for the celebration of reconciliation.

Whether used by itself or in conjunction with reconciliation, this ritual makes a beautiful ceremony. It has helped me to let go of unnecessary baggage and to experience healing and reconciliation. It's one of many treasures of my Native American heritage that has lightened my journey. I pass it on in the hope it will lighten yours, too.

22

In my travels in recent years, I have noticed an increasing number of children flying alone, some so young the airlines make them wear tags with names and destinations so they won't get lost. Some of these children, I found, come from divorced parents who shuttle them back and forth. I met Bill this way. During the five years I lived in western Montana, I would see him on flights to and from Denver. When I first ran into him, he was seven years old. He lived with his father in Montana and flew back and forth to his mother in Chicago. On holidays – Thanksgiving, Christmas, Easter, the start of vacations – Bill traveled. On one of his trips, we sat in the same row. He told me he hated these trips. "I just feel jerked around all the time," he said. He felt neither of his parents wanted him because both had new families. His mother insisted he visit, but Bill suspected she repeated her invitations to keep from feeling guilty.

I saw him several times. I remember once he was returning from his mother's at Christmas. I asked, "Did you have a nice Christmas, Bill?" "Oh," he said, "things, just things. That's all we had for Christmas. Things."

After moving to Oakland, I did not see him for a year or so. One night in Denver I got off a plane from Oakland and, to my surprise, he did too. His mother had moved there, he explained. Now 13, he looked very grown up, but he was still unhappy about all the traveling. Soon he told me how he intended to *sue* his parents. I was startled. He had already seen a lawyer. He wanted the court to get him out from under his parents' control so he wouldn't have to travel so much.

"I bear the burden of this divorce," he said. "Everybody else is home for Thanksgiving, I'm flying. Everybody else is home for

51

Christmas, I'm flying. Everybody else is home for summer vacation, I'm flying. I'm always flying. I don't have any real friends. I'd like to stay in one place for a while."

He wanted to live with his grandparents, in Montana. Then he could stay home and have a normal life. That was his plan. I told him I had moved to Oakland and gave him my phone number and said he should call when he came again. I asked him for his number, but he didn't have just one. He had a list! He gave he his grandparents' number and then said he had a few others I could have, too: His mother's home, the place she worked, his father's home, the place he worked, his stepmother's work number, his stepfather's work number, and emergency numbers in two cities. The kid needed an address book!

He got on his plane and I got on mine. What a sad story, I thought. Was there anything salvific about it? Well, Bill was trying to solve his problem. From TV, he had learned about public defenders and had gone to see one to get help. He always struck me as likable and confident. Now he showed he had guts, too. He hadn't let his problem overwhelm him. His response to his situation gave me hope that he would find the home he wanted so badly. His parents had their own needs, of course, but they had him flying so much that he was up in the air more ways than one. Somehow, he managed to be "up" in the right way. I make that my prayer for all the kids I see flying alone these days.

Four Ways to Resurrection

23

I have taught a resurrection prayer to children with wonderful results. It also works well with adults who have a sense of playfulness. It makes a great Easter prayer, but because Christians are an Easter people, I think it timely year around for both young and old. I call it the Four-Way Resurrection prayer. I like it because it gets me in touch with the ordinary resurrections in life – things that lift me up and bring me back from the dead of the routine. Further, it helps me to relate these ordinary resurrections to Christ's resurrection. There are four steps or ways. Welcome God into each, and proceed as follows:

1) **Stand up.** Now that doesn't sound like much, I know, but if you think about it, it can become more than just a physical movement. In saying this prayer with children, I seat them and talk about our wonderful bodies and how great it is that we can stand up and more around. Then I tell them to "get up," and after they have done so, I invite them to think about what they have done, and how life contains many such upward movements – when you learn something, when you accomplish something, or when someone helps you. All these little resurrections point to the big one.

2) **Lift the spirit.** After you have got your body up, you want to make sure your spirit rises as well, thus broadening the experience of resurrection. "Lift your mind, lift your heart, as you have lifted your body," I tell the children. "Feel yourself being swept up into the spirit and the love of your family and loved ones. See yourself being lifted to the higher things of life and into the mysterious presence of God who surrounds us."

3) **Reach for the sky.** You've stood up, you've lifted your spirit. Now it's the body's turn again. Indeed, if you're in the spirit of the prayer, the body will want to do more. "It's one thing

to stand up," I say to the kids. "It's another to stand up consciously, lift your arms and throw your head back. This is standing tall, this is raising all of your body."

4) **Shout about it.** Now you've had three resurrection experiences, each lifting you up, each a richer experience than the one before, each a reminder of the final, great resurrection. It's time to raise your voice. I tell the kids: "You're standing, you've raised your mind and heart, and your arms are up and your head is back and you're standing tall. Now it's time to sound off, to shout 'Alleluia' or 'I love you' or whatever you want to say to the Lord."

Kids got into this prayer quickly. It can get pretty animated and vocal and spirited. But you don't have to be a child or a member of a group to do this prayer. Often, I say the prayer by myself. I like saying it in the morning when I get up. In summer, it works well outdoors on the grass or under a tree.

You can make your own adaptations. At first you may feel a little silly or self-conscious. But stick with it. Like me, I believe you will discover resurrection in your life, first in these four ordinary ways, and then in many more.

Miss Innocent's Lesson

24

When I was in the third grade, my youngest brother, Jim, who was four years old, would meet me after school. He would bring our dog and the three of us would walk home together. One day I cleaned the erasers and got outside late. I didn't see Jim, and I became concerned, because he was so faithful. At home, I found him crying.

He said a big kid had shoved him, knocked him down and jumped on him. Right away I knew who did it. It had to be Jack, a bully in the seventh grade much bigger and older than other kids in his class. He had been held back two or three times. Jack always picked on little kids. I got mad about it, but never did anything. This time though, I resolved not to let him get by, because he had picked on Jim, who had become my spiritual brother on our walks home, and who, after all, was a four-year-old.

I told Jim not to tell anybody and to meet me at school the next day, just like always. I said I had a plan. I told Jim to play on the school ground after school. I would hide behind the lilac bush next to the third grade classroom. When Jack showed up, I would take care of him.

Jack took the bait. He stood well over a foot taller than I did and weighed I don't know how much more, but when he appeared and started pushing Jim around again, I turned into a tiger. When Jack had his back to me, I jumped him, knocked him down in the cinders, sat on his back and hit him as hard as I could. I got him pretty good. Then he threw me off, jumped up, and yelling and screaming, took off.

I felt sure he wouldn't bother us any more. The next evening when I got home my mother wanted to see me. I was about to learn what the word "provocation" meant. She said she had a warrant charging me with beating up Jack "without provocation." It ordered me to appear in court.

When court day came, my mother got me up early and fixed me up real pretty in a little white dress, white stockings and black patent leather slippers. She even put ribbons in my hair, and in those days I *never* wore ribbons. Inside the courthouse, we came upon a fat fellow in a cowboy outfit. He sat in a chair with the front legs off the floor and the back propped up against the wall. My mother asked for the number of our courtroom. The man motioned toward a door next to him.

Inside, the judge, a big man with an artificial leg, lumbered in, climbed a couple steps onto a platform. He plopped into a chair behind the bench with a great big circling motion. To a little kid, he looked like God. The judge called me and my mother up on one side of the bench, Jack and his mother on the other. Jack looked terrible. He had a black eye, a scratched face and a bandage around his head. I stood in my white finery, holding my mother's hand, not a scratch on me.

"Is this the one who beat you up like that?" the judge asked. Pointing, Jack said, "That's her! That's her!" The judge studied us one by one – Jack, his mother (a rawboned woman who made it unnecessary to guess where Jack got his size); my mother, just over five feet, and me, Little Miss Innocent. "Are you sure? the judge asked. "That's her, that's her." The judge looked at me and then at Jack, and pretty soon he started laughing. He couldn't stop. When he'd wind down and try to talk, he'd start all over again. Finally, he waved mother and me out the door, without ever getting himself under control enough to say a word.

Mother pivoted and led me out. I remember she gave the man outside the courtroom a proper little nod, and, as she did, the front legs of his chair plopped forward onto the floor, making a loud noise echoing down the hallway as we headed for the door. At home, my mother said, "Jo, there are other ways than fighting." I wish I could say I believed her at the time. I guess it took about 10 years before I did. And, to be honest, I have had to persuade myself again from time to time, because, as this story shows, fighting seems to work. No wonder we find it such an attractive way to solve our problems.

Greening Your Spirit

25

Hildegard of Bingen, a German abbess who was born in 1098 and died in 1179, earned a well deserved reputation as a beautiful and talented woman. She was an artist, a poet, a singer, a composer, a teacher, a mystic, an abbess, a saint. All in all, a wonderful gift from God.

She said many insightful things about living as Christians. I find most helpful her observation that we keep ourselves "green in the Spirit." By that, she meant we should keep our spirit fresh and alive, the way spring is alive with new life and growth. Hildegard offered three ways of doing that.

1) Know your tradition and study your scriptures. Stay close to your stories, she said, whether written or oral. This includes the rituals and rites we use to celebrate our stories and to pass them on.

I think I can say I have tried to do that and it has helped me to keep "green." Take the beautiful images of the creation stories in Genesis. They contain so much beauty and delight. God creates us from clay. What a wonderful image for making us one with the earth. It really makes the earth our mother. God breathes life into us. Somehow God's life, breath, spirit become our life, breath, spirit. Can't you just see God doing these things? And can't you see God taking delight in doing them? Our scriptures tell many stories of God's delight and joy. There are humorous ones, too – for example, Balaam and his talking ass, and Sarah laughing behind the tent. No wonder Hildegard urges us to know our story.

2) Be in touch with creation. Hildegard said we become poverty-stricken if we don't have a love affair with creation. She

had in mind not just the trees and plants and the flowers, but the stars and the moon and sun – everything. Touch creation, connect with it, she said. If you touch creation, you relate to it. If you relate to creation, you will not dominate it the way so many of us do these days, saying, in effect, "I'll take what I want and use it the way I want. Someone else can come along and clean up my mess."

This relational approach to creation is very Franciscan. St. Francis of Assisi – born, by the way, not far from where Hildegard died – said things like, "My brother, the sun, who leads the day into glory, my sister, the moon, who keeps the earth lit at night." These words reflect a relationship with creation. In contrast, we boss the earth, and bossing does not lead to good relationships. How many of us can say, "My Mother, the earth; my Father, the sky," and really mean it? No wonder our spirituality lacks "green."

3) Reflect on your own experiences. Hildegard advised connecting our experience to everything else, in particular to our tradition and scripture, and to creation. Each of us has a story, each of us is a story. We must tell these stories not only to each other, but to ourselves. In fact, I believe that before we can tell our stories to others, we must tell them to ourselves. That shows why reflecting on our own experience becomes so important.

I try to do that. For example, my parents worked at nurturing their children. While they did not have much in the way of money or possessions, they gave what they had, and they did so without strings attached. This forms an important part of my own story, my own experience, and I find myself thinking about it frequently. Doing so has helped me to see creation in the same way. Wherever I look, creation gives, provides, nurtures. And, not surprisingly, I have developed the image of God as well.

Hildegard's three guidelines have helped to keep me "greening in the Spirit." They have also enabled me to help others to do the same. A major reason: Simply and clearly they bring out the delight and excitement of living. Perhaps you, too, will find them a refreshing way of adding a little green to your life, to your spirit.

Stepping Out, Stepping In

26

When I was a child, my mother taught me many prayers from Native American traditions that I still find meaningful. Without fail, I have found these prayers have enriched my faith and prayer as a Roman Catholic. I call one of these the Three Step Prayer.

Though not part of her own tribe's heritage, my mother picked up this prayer from other Native Americans. Many tribes still use it today. My experience shows the prayer works as a Christian prayer, an individual prayer, a family prayer, and a creation prayer.

The prayer goes by various names among the tribes. One, for instance, calls it the Way of the Steps. Normally, Native Americans say it in the morning. In some ways, the prayer reminds me of Christian morning prayer, or the morning offering. There are three steps. In the first, you focus on the day ahead, in the second, on yourself, and in the third, on the mystery in life.

As with most Native American prayers, it places a strong emphasis on the earth. Because of that, I believe the prayer works best when said outdoors, although with a little imagination it can be used anywhere. Usually, you face the east, toward the rising sun, preferably in a spot with a vista. You begin by standing still and centering yourself.

You may vary the size and type of steps. You may take the steps with or without words. Native Americans usually perform the prayer without words, as is customary with many Indian rituals. I go through the prayer without words, too, although for beginners words might be helpful.

The first step signifies going into the day ahead. You step out and greet and accept the day and everything that you will receive during the day. If done outdoors, a panoramic view of earth and sky could suggest the notion of accepting everything that comes your way. A sample prayer for this first step:

> "O Great God (or Great Spirit, if you want to use Native American language), you give me this day as a special gift. In taking this step into the day, I accept everything it will bring, whether part of my plan or not. Teach me to accept every gift that comes my way today. Help me to use each gift wisely, to love my brothers and sisters, and to care for my Mother the Earth."

The second step expresses the idea of entering into yourself. A prayer to go with this step might say: "O Great God (or Great Spirit), you created me as I am. In taking this step, I accept myself as a I am, as I have been in the past, and as I will be in the future. I ask that today I will be true to the way you made me. Help me to walk respectfully on my Mother the Earth so none of its plants will be crushed. Help me to walk into people's lives in the same way, so none will be bruised."

Step three suggests going into mystery. With this step, a prayer might be: "O Great God (or Great Spirit), you created me and everything around me with a sense of mystery. I now step into that mystery and put my arms around it. Help me to accept the things of this day I do not, and cannot, understand. Help me to use the encounters with mystery to draw nearer to you, to my brothers and sisters, and to all you have made."

While similar to the morning offering, for so long a meaningful Christian prayer, the emphasis in this prayer differs slightly. In the morning offering, we offer our day to God. Often, however, we don't seem to have much to offer except our own all too meager efforts. The Three Step Prayer emphasizes accepting what God gives us. If we offer *that* back to God, we really have something to give.

All of this makes the Three Step Prayer another example of Native American prayer enriching my Christian prayer. I suspect it might do the same for you.

Four Days
of Thanksgiving

27

Thanksgiving. It means different things to different people. For some, it brings an extended holiday weekend. For others, it becomes a day of thanks that may or may not include church. For still others, the day centers on family and a big meal, with vague notions of Indians and pilgrims in the background.

For Native Americans, Thanksgiving often turns into a sad day of remembering what they lost because another culture with different values and customs took over their land. Some younger tribal members use the day for protests calling attention to their grievances.

I have found that my Native American background enriches Thanksgiving for me. The traditions of the Seneca Iroquois Tribe, in particular, embody many profound thanksgiving insights and rituals. This tribe celebrates one ritual of thanks lasting four full days. The ritual's formal order consists of storytelling, teachings, silence, singing, drumming, chanting, rest, special foods (including the tribe's sacred berry, the strawberry), and, finally, remembering all the things for which to be thankful.

To help with this remembering, the ritual features 18 special chants of thanks – for people, the earth, plants, water, trees, animals, birds, the "sisters," (special powers that help people take care of themselves and look after each other), the wind, thunder-ers (powers that bring rain), the sun, the moon, the stars, the Four Beings (powers that bring enlightenment and strength), Handsome Lake (a member of the tribe who spread Christian values), and, finally, the Creator.

In this ritual, the chanting of the story of Thanksgiving might begin this way: "Now the people have gathered to give thanks. In the early time, the Sky Dwellers (beings in Native American origin stories who came to earth and helped populate it) told us we must move about the earth with love. They said the first thing we must do when we meet one another is be thankful for each other. Above all, we must relate to the earth as our mother, who supports all, even our very feet." It continues litany-like in this fashion.

I like the ritual's this-world focus. I think that makes it worth passing on to the Christian community in this country. We Americans, including many of us Christians, take what we have for granted. Or, we think that we have earned everything we have. Often, we fail to see that these things – especially the important things – come from the earth, from each other, and, when all is said and done, from God. In other words, they are gifts. Often, Christians do see these gifts come from God. And we thank God for them. But frequently we fail to appreciate the fact that God gives us these gifts, including life itself, through creation. In other words, we still think of the Creator as completely separated from creation, and, by doing that, we perpetuate the old dichotomies that have plagued our past.

As you can see from the Seneca Iroquois ritual of thanksgiving, Native American people have less difficulty with this. Somehow, they keep their focus on this world longer than many of us Christians, while, at the same time, still relating it to the Creator. Note this, for example, in the 18 thanksgiving chants of this ritual – the first 17 concern creation and finally the last one mentions the Creator.

I don't suggest you duplicate this Native American ritual of thanksgiving – can you imagine yourself giving thanks for four solid days? I recount it to show the profound sense of thanksgiving among Native Americans. In part, I believe that stems from the fact they avoided a major dichotomy between the spiritual and the material.

As a result, Native American ways can enrich not only our Thanksgiving but all celebrations of thanks, for at bottom, all of life's gifts come from the Creator through creation.

28

I spent two weeks working as a volunteer during the big fire in the hills in and near Oakland, California – the one that destroyed about 5,000 homes and took at least 25 lives in the fall of 1991. Living through that tragedy brought home to me some important lessons for our everyday lives. While I know these lessons, I tend to forget them. Now that I recall them, I see they form the basis of a pretty good spirituality.

1) Things don't make the person. Many fire victims lost absolutely every earthly thing they had – house, cars, keepsakes, etc. One woman went back to her house and found only a cup, one cup. Many didn't find even that. I saw and talked with some. Many expressed shock. Some despaired or came very close. Yet, they still had life. They still had each other. Seeing that helped me to realize again that the things we have don't make us who we are, even though we often live, work and spend as if they did.

2) Living requires starting over. Because most victims of this fire lost everything, they had no choice but to begin again. At first, they all came together – and held on. Soon, however, they talked of building again, not only their homes but their communities. I could not help but see how often we must start over in daily life – a job turns sour, a marriage breaks up, a spouse dies. In a sense, we must start over every morning. If we don't start over, we die, or soon will. Seeing the fire victims start over helped me to see we must do it too.

3) People are good. Everybody pitched in and helped out. Even hard-hearted businesses. Safeway and Lucky – two giant food chains – brought in trucks of food. Money rolled into the Red Cross center where I worked. The 300 kids I helped care for needed underwear and socks. When I went to get some,

merchants donated most of what was needed. On one such excursion, I came back with 400 T-shirts! In daily life, we forget people's essential goodness. We even seem to forget it of ourselves. But this tragic fire helped me to see that this goodness remains, not only within myself but other people as well.

4) We depend on each other. At the shelter, I worked mainly with the children. Basic things – things we take for granted – became the biggest challenge in caring for them: brushing teeth and bathing, preparing food and finding a place to eat, cleaning clothes, setting up rest rooms, getting a place to sleep, etc. We really worked together to come up with makeshift arrangements for these basics necessities. When we have these necessities, they seem to come to us automatically. In fact, they do not. We depend on each other for them. Think for a moment how we get our water, food, shelter, etc. Without a succession of people, most of whom we do not know and will never meet, we would not have these things. So, we depend on each other not only in crises, but all of the time.

5) Suffering remains a mystery. I don't know why such tragedies happen. I see it as a natural disaster – after five years of drought a fire like this just waiting to happen. As people often do, some spoke of it as an "act of God," but I have no sense that God somehow caused the fire. Again and again I saw people in pain and agony drawing on an inner strength, a strength that can best be explained, I think, by our belief in divine presence in and among people. Consequently, instead of seeing tragedies such as this as divine thunderbolts, I think it more accurate to speak of God suffering with people – and, after all, isn't that the message of the crucifixion?

Our tendency to forget the obvious lessons tragedies teach about living, I suspect, accounts for the fact that our lives often turn into tragedies.

29

I don't think about the Holy Land much except during Lent, and, in particular, Holy Week and Easter. Then, I find myself, especially in my prayer, preoccupied with the place where Jesus spent his final days. And my reflections usually center on my one – and only – visit there.

It took place more than 20 years ago. Ten of us Sisters of St. Francis of Milwaukee spent six weeks walking through the Holy Land. We went, in the style of St. Francis, as poor praying pilgrims. It was definitely a low-budget affair. For me, the highlight came during an encounter with a "beggar." I relive it every year during Lent-Easter, and I always come away renewed in my awareness of what it means to follow Christ.

We began the walk with Jerusalem as our destination. As we walked, we became increasingly aware of following in the footsteps of Jesus as he headed toward his final crisis. After reaching Jerusalem, we spent days there. Each morning, about five o'clock, I got up, took my Bible and prayed in a square near one of the great mosques, a site of religious significance to Muslims, Jews and Christians.

One morning, a very, very old man approached me. He looked more like a shriveled up dwarf than a man. His back had a hump; his head and feet were bare. He wore only a dirty white rag wrapped around his body. When he smiled, I saw he had two teeth. He held out a bowl. At first, I thought he wanted money. Then I realized he was offering food. I looked in the bowl and saw an awful looking mixture of chicken bones, an animal skin, grain, and a milky-looking liquid. Smiling, he pulled a dirty little spoon from the bowl and, with anticipation, invited me to help myself.

I didn't know what to do. The stuff in the bowl looked awful. It didn't smell any better. Finally, I tried the spoon but got very little of the mixture out of the bowel with it. I experienced a momentary sense of relief. But I could see the man still looking at me. His sense of anticipation showed no signs of diminishing. Slowly, I put the bowl to my mouth and half drank and half ate – and half gagged. When I finished, I smiled and he smiled, and then – and I'll *never* forget this – he offered it to me again! I forced myself to take another helping. We smiled and nodded in a kind of semi-bow – and he walked on, thank goodness.

Almost immediately, three guards descended upon me. I thought they had come to nab me for violating a code of some kind. But they commended me for taking the beggar's food. The man frequently came to the square to offer people food, they said, but no one had ever accepted it until I did. As we talked, the guards, who seemed touched by what I had done, asked if they could do anything for me. I said I wanted to get into the Mosque, then closed to visitors. No, no, they said only dignitaries could get in and they had to have a pass from the security chief. Would they take me to see him? Reluctantly, they did. Reluctantly, too, he gave me a pass.

Inside, I saw a thing of beauty – lovely tile and windows, the words of the Koran gracefully carved into the walls. Worshippers said morning prayer. As I watched, I had a profound sense of the holy. I would call it a religious experience. Afterward, I insisted on going back and thanking the chief. He expressed surprise, saying no one had returned before to thank him for a pass.

Over the years, in reliving this experience, I have had these reflections:

1) Following in the footsteps of Jesus will lead us to the poor;
2) the poor will lead us to God, as my acceptance of this poor man led me to a religious experience in the Mosque;
3) even the lowliest among us have gifts to share and, I suspect, their gifts often become the ones we really need, even though we almost automatically discount them;

4) nothing surpasses sharing food, in church or out, for experiencing our oneness with each other and with God, and
5) you don't have to go to the Holy Land to experience God, for thanks to the resurrection and the sending of the Spirit, God is present in everyone, especially the poor and outcast, where we live or where Jesus lived.

Next Lent and Easter when you try to renew what it means to follow Christ, I suggest hanging around the poor and accepting them. As the meaning of the experience sinks in, and starts changing your life, don't forget to return and give thanks.

30

In the years immediately after the Second Vatican Council, Catholics sometimes measured how far along their parishes had come in renewing worship by how well, and how willingly, they participated in the exchange or kiss of peace.

These days some Catholics – and I would include myself – gauge how much people have renewed their spiritual life by the degree they have integrated creation spirituality, which I will summarize, too briefly to be sure, as seeing creation as a blessing and believing the Creator present in it and operating through it.

During the Easter season, I often find myself recalling a tribe of Native Americans way ahead of most of us on both counts. They developed a unique ritual of peace many years before the Vatican Council, and their rite showed a profound awareness of what we today call creation spirituality.

The tribe is the Papago. They are the most Catholic of any tribe I know, about 95 per cent. They live 70 miles south of Tucson and share a border with Mexico. Though heavily Catholic, the Papagos did not always have a priest to preside at their worship. They developed a special ritual for the time when they did not have one. This ritual combines elements of creation spirituality and the rite of the kiss of peace.

The Papago carry out the ritual in the spring, when the desert bursts into bloom with flowers and color. On the appointed day, usually just before Easter, the people gather bunches of flowers and greenery – avoiding any that might prickle or injure – and carry them to church.

At the kiss of peace everyone springs into action! They run around throwing flowers at one another, pelting each other with petals and greenery and crying out, "Peace be to you! Beauty be in you!" When no one has flowers left, people gather them up from the floor and start all over again.

Sometimes the community singles out individuals for special honors. When that happens, the people dump baskets of flowers and greenery upon that person, signifying that this individual should be more deeply touched with beauty and peace because of their important role in and contribution to the community. When the liturgy ends, people do not run for brooms and sweep everything away. They leave all the evidence around for days. This keeps the memory alive. When other people come along and see the dying flowers, they wonder, "What kind of mess is this?" That provides a perfect opportunity to tell the story again.

If you have not seen this ritual, it may sound strange. But I don't see it as strange. On the contrary, I find it filled with meaning. The beautiful flowers – and their colors are endless – symbolize beauty, the beauty of creation. Pelting represents an effort to make each other aware of that beauty and to emphasize the point that each of us must accept it and be filled with it.

Further, the pelting suggests that people will not be at peace – with themselves, with each other, and with God – until they have developed an appreciation of nature's beauty. In this way, I think the ritual expresses the truth that you do not have peace until you have made peace with nature. You do not have peace apart from appreciating yourself as a part of creation. This connection enables us to see in a new way. Among other things, we find we can learn of the goodness of God from what God has made. Also, we find we can discover God present and working through all of creation. God does not work over or under or around creation but comes to us through it, especially through its beauty and mystery. In other words, creation truly reveals God and God's work.

Therefore, being in touch with creation puts us in touch with the Creator. The Papagos sense that and try to express it in their flower-pelting ritual. They see beauty. That leads them to nature. Nature leads them to God. In God they find peace, a peace they share with their flower ritual. I have participated in the Papagos' ritual. After the first time, I said to myself, "Now I know what the kiss of peace means."

Walking into the World

31

When I was between the ages of five and ten, my mother took us kids for prayer walks in the summertime after supper. We lived in a little town in southwestern Colorado and would walk into the countryside. There were ten of us – I had nine brothers – and she took one at a time. The rest of the kids and Daddy stayed home to wash the dishes. I remember those walks as very meaningful, though I confess at the beginning I had as much interest in getting out of dishes as I did in prayer walks.

Mother had a routine. We walked about a mile, without shoes, in silence, hand-in-hand. Usually, she talked only at the start, varying her remarks on this theme: "Look at the world. See what a wonderful world it is. All I want you to do is walk and be thankful. Thank God for the beautiful place we have to live."

Then we set out, my mother and I, down the dusty road, swinging our arms between us and running our bare feet through the red dirt. At some point, I would hold back and make my mother pull me along. I wanted to slow us down to make sure we didn't get back before the dishes were done. Sometimes Daddy and the boys dallied a bit.

Even though mother urged me to look around as we walked, I made my first connection with the earth through the sense of touch – through feeling the red sand with my bare feet. I noticed that, even though the days were usually hot and dry, the red sand always seemed cool and moist. I never did figure out why, but it gave me my first clue that the earth contained surprises and wonders.

In time, through these walks, I developed a wonderful sense of walking into the world, and the world, in turn, walking into me. I went out to the world. The world came into me. I became part of it. It became part of me. Somehow we became one. And I became one with the things in the world.

I developed this sense of oneness with the rabbits we saw. I liked the rabbits. They were quick, abundant, playful, always hopping around. As a little girl, I liked seeing myself as one of them. To this day, I think of myself as quick and playful as those rabbits. I learned about life from prairie dogs. They gave very good lessons about community. They popped in and out of their holes, always interacting with each other. They stood guard for one another and sounded warnings. I didn't have to watch long to learn the importance of home and family.

They taught another valuable lesson, one, I think, especially important for us as Christians. The prairie dogs seemed to have little or nothing. I did not think of them as attractive, as the rabbits. They lived on barren land that offered little. Yet, they lived a vibrant community life. They had little, yet they had so much.

Mountains beckoned me on these walks. On three sides, I could see wonderful peaks – majestic and beautiful, tall and challenging. I placed many of my hopes and dreams on those peaks. They came to represent goals for me. Later on, when I wanted something, I would often think of it in terms of those mountain peaks. "I can climb that," I would tell myself. I did that, for example, with my desire to become a teacher – every accomplishment along the way became another step up the mountain. I have no doubt this image helped me to make that dream come true. In the fourth direction, I saw wide open spaces. No mountains, just endless horizon. In my mind, this became my opening to the rest of the world, the outside world far beyond the dusty little place where I lived. One day, I would go beyond that horizon. When I did, I came upon another horizon. I went beyond that to another horizon. And beyond that to another. Life became an ever-shifting summit.

While my walks with my mother took place in silence, I heard a lot of talking. The world told me about itself, about myself, and about the mystery permeating everything, a mystery making us one. I got more out of those prayer walks than just getting out of doing dishes.

Three Great Teachers

32

John Steinbeck, the writer, said if you have two great teachers in your life, you should consider yourself blessed. I have had three and so consider myself unusually blessed.

First, Miss James. She taught me in second grade. At least 65, she was plump and unmarried, which made her an "old maid," a way of life looked down upon in those days. She had 83 of us in her classroom, an unbelievable number by today's standards. Yet, she turned our classroom into a magical place.

She made each of us feel important and talented. She made sure everybody knew everybody's virtues. She put a monthly calendar on the blackboard. One way or another, everyone made it onto the calendar – birthdays, achievements large and small, whatever happened. She named every kid best at something. I remember one cited as best at adjusting the shades to regulate the sunlight. That may not seem like much, but it contributed to the class. And it meant a lot to that kid. She named me best reader. When the weather prevented us from going out at recess, I got to read stories to the class.

One day while sitting in the back row, I said to myself, "I want to do to children's lives what Miss James does to ours. I want to make every kid feel important." That day I decided to become a teacher, which I later did, joining a religious community and teaching in Catholic schools for a number of years.

In the eighth grade, I met my second great teacher, Mrs. Grace Kuenneth. She expanded my horizons in every direction, including the notion of what it meant to teach. She could turn everything into an educational opportunity, whether in the classroom or not. I remember her doing that, for instance, when we redecorated the school gym. We seemed stumped as to what to do. "Be creative," she said. "Take responsibility."

She was great one-on-one. In our first conversation, she said she heard I wanted to teach. "Why not become an educator instead?" she asked. I asked the difference. "A teacher's place is the classroom, an educator's place is the world," she said. She explained that if I got a well-rounded education I could change my direction more easily, but if I concentrated on teaching I would probably spend all my life in a classroom.

I followed her advice. Later, after a number of satisfying years in the classroom, I did move on – to teach among my Native American people and to give lectures, workshops and retreats throughout the country and around the world.

Finally, I remember Sister Doris Hachmeister as a great teacher. A member of my own community, the Sisters of St. Francis of Assisi, in Milwaukee, I met her as a postulant, in her class on Shakespeare. I recall her saying she would not only teach us about Shakespeare, but about life. And she knew about life. She brought Shakespeare to life, she brought me to life, she brought all her students to life. She struck me as a very spiritual person, a seeker. She played a major role in my formation for three years. During that time, she confirmed my instinct that nothing exceeds spiritual growth in excitement. She did that mainly through making demands: "Write this, seek this, find this, tell this, do that." She made us dig. You couldn't get by with saying something like "living as a Christian is great." She pushed you to tell how and why.

I had many other fine teachers, too. Why do I single out these three? Because in some mysterious way, they changed me. As a result, I saw I wanted to teach. I saw education meant learning life in the world. I saw that living centers in a spiritual quest. They expanded my notion of teaching. Whether in the classroom or not, we all teach, we all touch lives, we all change lives. In that way, we become blessings for each other. We might even make someone's list of three great teachers.

33

How Many Valentines?

In the fourth grade, I started making and sending Valentines to the pope. I have sent one every year since, and, as I write this, I am on my fifty-third in a row. My mother's suggestion got me started. In my school, as I think in many schools, kids gave each other Valentines. My class had about 80 kids in it. I could not begin to make or buy each a Valentine.

Out of the blue, my mother asked, "Why don't you send the pope a Valentine?" I did not get very excited about that. I already had too many names of my list. But she persuaded me, saying the pope probably did not get Valentines and would appreciate one. I made a Valentine for the pope, got his address from the priest who came to our mission church, and mailed it.

I still make the Valentines more or less as I did at the start. Usually, I draw something – birds, trees, flowers – and write a personal note wishing him well and expressing my affection. As I grew up, I remember, I made one change. I had the message translated to make sure he could read it. Years went by. I made and sent a Valentine without fail. I never got a response. I wondered if the pope actually got my Valentines. To try to increase the chances, I started using three envelopes. On the outside of the first, I wrote, "Confidential." On the second, I put, "Strictly Confidential," and, on the third, I said, "Open at Your Own Risk!"

Then – surprise! – an envelope from the Vatican. Inside I found a handwritten note saying, "Thank you for the Valentine. First one I ever received." It was signed "John XXIII." I can still see the handwriting, a little uneven and running downhill. I have not received a response since then, but I don't mind, because making and sending the cards does more for me than for the pope. Expressing love and support to a person always makes me feel good. In addition, it serves as a reminder to me of the importance of communicating by mail.

A card, a note, a letter, a thoughtful remembrance can make or break a person's day. As a one-time student and former teacher of English, I have always had a love for the word, for language. I have come to see that such notes written with love, and accompanied by a brief prayer, can become a Word made Flesh.

Over the years, I have made it a practice of pausing before writing and mailing a letter. I say a brief prayer for the person receiving it and ask that my message will contribute to the person's well-being. On receiving a letter myself, I often pause before opening it and ask that I will be open to the one sending it and to any message God might be addressing to me.

I think we would do well to do this with all our correspondence, including that of work and business. That may sound a little strange at first. It may seem removed from our concerns as Christians. But I believe otherwise. Stop and think for a minute about the effect that work and business correspondence have on the world and on people's lives.

Indeed, such seemingly "secular" correspondence results in profound spiritual effects. Each day, countless pieces of business mail affect what we do with food, water, clothing, shelter, medical care, all the gifts and resources God gives us. If we handled this correspondence with more care – and a prayer now and then – we would not confine the sending of Valentines to one day a year. We would send them every day.

Oh, by the way, if you want to join me next year in sending the pope a Valentine, I suggest getting it in the mail by the middle of January. His address is: Pope John Paul II, Apostolic Palace, 00120 Vatican City State.

People Who Are Prayer

34

I just returned from Ecuador, a small country between Colombia and Peru on the Pacific side of South America. I spent 10 days there giving a retreat to priests and parish staff members. They told me the retreat went well and that I helped them with their spiritual life. But I don't want to write about that. I want to tell how the people live and how deeply they affected *my* spiritual life. I can sum it up by saying they became prayer for me.

By that I mean, all I have to do now – a week after getting back – is think about them, see them in my mind, and I know I was in the presence of people who live in the presence of God. They would laugh at this, of course, but they reflect God as we think of saints as doing. While with them, I responded to the God who shines through them. And I still do that. Now you can see what I mean by saying they became prayer for me.

If I tell you more I think it will become clearer. Furthermore, you could very well see God present in people you know who live in the same way in similar circumstances. If you do, do not be surprised if they become prayer for you, as the people of Ecuador have for me.

I have traveled abroad before but I have never seen such poverty. One day, for example, I ate in the home of a family of five. They had a hut no more than 10 feet square. They built it out over the water because they could not afford to build on land. The floor had big holes in it. Big enough for a baby to fall through, I thought, as we ate.

Little or nothing seems to work in the country. You can't pick up the telephone and expect to get a call through. Worse, the political system does not work – at least not for the people I met. The water is dirty. The sewers are clogged. The roads are rough. Moreover, they would have no services at all without church support. The people can put their trust in little. For example, they told me the bottled water sold in stores often has been scooped up in someone's back yard.

The social and economic system never lets up on them, not even when death comes. During my stay two persons died in one parish. Aside from sorrow and mourning, these deaths brought another problem: How to get money for the funeral? Funeral directors will not release bodies for burial until the funeral expenses have been paid. The parish contributed the Sunday morning collection. I gave all the Ecuadorian money I had. Eventually they got enough money together.

In spite of these conditions the people remain terrific. They work hard. Many weave, making hats, coats, dresses and other clothing. I went to an open-air market. No one pressured me, even though I knew that if they did not sell they would not eat. Instead, they offered their wares in a gracious manner. I bought a jacket from a man. He had made it himself, and done a good job, too. He asked 80,000 sucres, about $20. My hosts had given me 100,000 to spend. I decided I would buy the jacket and give him the remaining 20,000 as well. When I did he burst into tears.

The people's love for their children impressed me most. In the midst of all the poverty and dirt, I never saw a dirty-faced kid. The kids might have to walk in mud up to their ankles, but they always wore clean clothes – often white shirts and dresses. I never saw a child who looked hungry. These people could not make a living and raise their children without constant work and sacrifice. Yet, they always seemed to have time for prayer. When they found out I was a religious sister, they came up to me on the street and asked me to pray with them and for them.

By now you can see why these people became prayer for me. They did so much with so little. In that, I saw God's grace working among them. Don't forget now my reason for telling this story. You can find people like this in your life, too.

80

The Moistures of Life

35

I have lived through two major droughts. The first came in the late 1970s and early 1980s, in Arizona. I went through the second a decade later in California, where I still live. In going through these droughts, I discovered one thing about water – nothing can make its importance as clear as a shortage of it.

Every day brought reminders of the lack of water. In California, officials issued a steady stream of appeals to cut down on water use. At times, they prohibited watering lawns. In Arizona, I remember people turning each other in for violating a ban against washing cars. I also recall cattle eating cactus because they could find nothing else.

When I was a child in the desert Southwest, my mother used to tell me not to pass a drinking fountain without taking a drink. Water is precious, she said, and you never know when the fountain will run dry. Sometimes, during the droughts, it seemed as if my mother's saying had come true. I confess I passed up few water fountains during the droughts. Sometimes, I even went out of my way for one.

This focus on water, or the lack of it, had one positive effect. It did wonders for my prayer. I could hardly avoid reflecting on Yahweh liberating the Israelites through the Red Sea. Or, God identifying Jesus as his beloved Son as he emerged from the Jordan River. Or my own baptism. One biblical scene involving water became a favorite of mine: Jesus' encounter with the Woman at the Well. I never tired of hearing Jesus say to her, and to me, that he offered the living water of eternal life. Echoing my mother's advice about drinking fountains, I urge you never to pass by this story without drinking from it – not because the water in the story is scarce and may run out, but because it is so plentiful and life-giving. As a Native American, I also drew upon the tribal traditions in my reflections on water. Many tribes' traditions include what they call the "moistures of life." These moistures do not refer to water as you find it in nature, such as a lake or a river, but to the water in us, in our bodies. Thus, the use of the term "moistures."

There are four major moistures. First comes tears, the moisture of compassion. In reflecting on this moisture, I became aware again of an old truth – that compassion makes possible our relationships with each other. Further, I could see another old truth – that God relates to us with compassion. In a sense, that summarizes the story of Jesus. Finally, I saw, too that without God's compassion, we would be dead, as dead as land without water.

The tribal traditions name sweat as the second moisture. It is the moisture of working, of suffering, and of serving. In my reflections on sweat, I began to see it as a symbol of laying down our lives for each other and of sharing the gifts God has given us.

The third and fourth moistures may be a bit delicate for many of us Christians, for we have to a large extent, I'm afraid, separated our bodies from spirituality. Native Americans did not do that and their traditions remain bodily, more earthy. And, I would add more real, too.

In any event, the third moisture in the tribal traditions is that of the relieving the body. In a word, urine. To me, in my reflections, this became an important symbol of purification, not only of the body, but of my whole being. In time, I also made it a symbol of purifying myself in another way – by considering what I took into my body as well as what I eliminated from it. In this way, I made a connection with fasting as a form of purification.

The fourth moisture in this tradition is sexual, both male and female moistures. These moistures, of course, make possible the expressions of love and the procreation of life. In my reflections, this led me to such rich notions as our role as co-creators with God and, further, that in creating us male and female, God created us in the divine image and likeness.

The tribal traditions also speak of a fifth moisture, of somewhat lesser rank than the others. It is spit. The mouth needs spit in order to speak. It cannot form words with breath alone. It also needs moisture to speak a word. In reflecting on this, I began to see it as very biblical. The imagery of the opening chapter of Genesis even seems to suggests that breath and water helped to form God's word. It says, in verse two, that "a mighty wind swept over the waters," and then goes on to say that God spoke the words of creation.

These are ways that water has served as a cleansing and refreshing fountain of prayer for me. I think you will find it will satisfy your thirst as well. I urge you not to pass it up.

Remembering Cesar

36

I first met Cesar Chavez 21 years ago. I was doing graduate work and teaching at UCLA at the time. Dorothy Day had come to Los Angeles for the opening of the new Catholic Worker House, and, finding it a bit too noisy for the private retreat she wanted to make, she asked if she might stay with me in my apartment and make her retreat there. I said yes, if she would tell me about her life and experiences over supper each evening. She agreed, and so for the next eight evenings Dorothy talked and I listened.

One night she talked about Cesar Chavez' efforts to organize California's poor, migrant farm workers. When she found out I had not met him, she said I really should. In fact, she said, as a teacher of prayer and spirituality, I could help with the spiritual side of the farm worker struggle. Cesar always wanted help with that, she said. She arranged a meeting.

A few days later, a friend and I drove the 100 or so miles north to La Paz, near Keene, where Cesar and his wife, Helen, lived. They had a simple home. I found it hard to believe 10 people – they had eight children – lived in the house. Nothing about the house stood out except a barbed wire fence, put up to provide protection for Cesar, who received repeated threats against his life in those days.

In going over their needs, Cesar said he wanted help with celebrating the eucharist, which his union members regarded as important. They needed vestments and something besides a coffee mug or a Styrofoam cup for use as a chalice during their field masses. Later, I borrowed a beautiful chalice – it even had a diamond in it – from a friend. I also got vestments from a priest who, to say the least, was not at all friendly to Cesar's cause.

During a supper of pinto beans, I asked Helen and Cesar how, in the middle of such a difficult struggle, they maintained their sanity. How could they raise a family, establish a credit union, deal with the strife – including a barbed wire fence and guard dogs – and still maintain peace? After a pause, Helen answered that she and Cesar got up every morning at 4:30 and prayed for an hour. She said the rosary and read scripture, he meditated. Then, and only then, she said, did they feel prepared to begin the day.

I remembered this meeting fondly when I heard that Cesar had died unexpectedly, at 66 years of age. I remembered other meetings, too, including those that led to four members of my religious community – the Sisters of St. Francis of Assisi, in Milwaukee – working with the United Farm Workers, two for more than 10 years, two for about 20.

As I look back on Cesar, I see him as a man who seemed to anticipate three of the great spiritual movements of our time. First, he acted out of a lay spirituality. Cesar was a layman, the father of eight. Yet, he didn't wait for the church authorities to take the lead in helping the farm workers. Indeed, he led the church. He did not rely on the church for financial support, either. Instead, in faith, he stepped out on his own, and, in doing so, became an outstanding example of a modern Christian in the world. Though often overlooked on this score, Helen should not be, for she played a significant role in organizing and running the Farm Workers credit union.

Second, Cesar became the first to organize the last of the workers in the U.S. to be unionized, the farm workers. Unions had organized every other segment of society, but no one had bothered about the migrant poor, who pick the fruit and vegetables for our tables. Further, Cesar did his organizing in a very sophisticated way, following the non-violent approach of Jesus, Gandhi and King. In doing do, he pioneered the nonviolent way that must, I believe, become *the* way for settling disputes.

Third, Cesar sounded the alarm on pesticides. Chemicals, he said, endangered the health and safety of farm workers as well as consumers. In this, he anticipated the ecological movement and its spiritual manifestation, creation spirituality or eco-spirituality.

In recalling Cesar and what he did, I am struck by the fact that I was introduced to him as someone who might help him and his cause spiritually. Of course, he helped me and my spirituality far more than I helped him. I think that will turn out to be true of all of us.

The Pogo Prayer

37

I got an invitation the other day to speak at the 1994 Los Angeles Religious Education Congress. It reminded me of an appearance there 15 years ago. I remember it well because I received my best compliment in 32 years of traveling around teaching prayer.

I would speak to a couple hundred grade school children, I thought. Instead, I got several thousand. Right away, I knew I had to shift gears. What will work with a small group won't work with a large one. I needed to keep that many kids active. What would get them to move, yet stay in the same place – besides jumping up and down, of course? "Ah, that's it!" I said to myself, "I'll get them to jump up and down. It'll be more fun than pogo sticks."

I had part of what I needed. Now, if I could make connections with prayer, I would be all set. As a former teacher, I knew kids often did not feel appreciated. That would be a way of reaching them. Perhaps I could get them to appreciate each other. Appreciation got me thinking about being thankful. Perhaps I could get them to be thankful for what they had and for each other. And, jumping up and down could be a way of expressing it. The higher they jumped, the more they would show their appreciation and thankfulness. It wouldn't even take any words!

The kids filed into a huge auditorium, in seats rising up on both sides. I stood in between, on a stage built for the occasion, with a microphone in each direction. I asked the two sides to stand and face each other. Did they feel unappreciated? Yes! Did they appreciate each other? Yes! Were they thankful for each other? Yes! Were they thankful for what they had received, from their families, from teachers, from God? Yes! Yes! Yes!

Now, could they express this thankfulness by jumping up and down? Yes! I faced one side, jumping with them, then the other, jumping with them. Back and forth, higher and higher. They got into it. They turned it into a natural high. I started telling them their jumping symbolized God calling them to rise up, to resurrection. I said it represented their living a new life, even though, as it went on, I began to suspect it might cost me my own!

When I finally got them stopped, a boy – he turned out to be a sixth grader – jumped up on the stage, handed me his program and asked me to autograph it, because, he said, "This was better than a baseball game." I thought so at the time and I still think so today – that is the best compliment I have received in my years of teaching prayer. If you don't think so, just remember what baseball can mean a sixth grade boy.

Since then, I have taught the "pogo prayer" to kids around the country. They love it. Recently, I went to a parish in New Jersey where I had taught it three years ago. The first thing the kids said: "We want to do the pogo prayer." Not long ago I learned one generation passed it on to another. An abbot I know told me his nieces and nephews, who had learned the Pogo Prayer from me, did it with their children.

I have learned a lot about prayer from doing the Pogo Prayer. We can learn prayer from anyone, even and perhaps especially, from those we teach. When we pray we respond to life and to the One who gives life. Further, that response, in the first instance, naturally becomes a response of thanks for the gifts we have received and for other people. Prayer does not take many words; in fact, often the fewer the better.

Some of the time, indeed, much of the time, prayer becomes a time of joy. It produces a high. Prayer involves more than just the mind and the heart. The body must be part of it, too. Prayer has it ups and downs. That may sound prosaic, or even corny, but anyone who prays regularly knows "downs" come, in the same way a baseball player knows he will have slumps. Another lesson from the Pogo Prayer: There is nothing like praying together, especially in large groups. Last, and perhaps the best of all, I learned prayer can beat baseball.

The Fourteen Generations

38

Anyone who knows me knows my mother. She taught me many Native American traditions. These traditions have been teaching me about life and how to live it ever since. The concept of the Fourteen Generations remains one of the most broadening and challenging.

The idea seems simple – deceptively so: You pay reverence and respect to the seven generations that have gone before you and the seven generations that will come after you. According to this tradition, you keep seven generations, forward and back, in your mind and heart in everything you do, and live accordingly.

When my mother first told me about this, I responded primarily to the part concerning the seven generations who had gone before me. I liked the idea that for seven generations my ancestors had lived with me in mind. Knowing that, I felt I had been loved and cared for even before I arrived.

My mother explained that if I lived with my ancestors in my memory, it would give me a power I would not otherwise have. This proved correct. Being aware that these ancestors went ahead of me, and knowing they wanted to pass on to me what they had, has been a real gift. It gives me strength. Today we often speak of being empowered. Keeping the seven generations that preceded me in my memory does that. It empowers me.

While this may seem unusual to those of you not Native American, it should not seem strange to Roman Catholics, because of the teaching on the communion of saints. I can find a number of similarities, including the belief that those who have gone before still somehow connect with you and help you. My mother certainly saw the similarities. In fact, they helped to bring her, at age 25, into the Catholic Church.

As I grew so did my understanding of the Fourteen Generation tradition. As a child, I had been enamored with part of the tradition concerning those who had gone before me. But as an adult, I became more aware of keeping in my mind and heart the seven generations who will come after me. Now, instead of being on the receiving end, I moved to the giving side. Instead of being empowered, I saw myself as trying to empower. Instead of being imagined (as the seven generations before me had done), I tried to imagine those who would come for seven generations after me. Just as they wanted to pass on to me what they had, I now wanted to pass on what I had to those who would follow me.

And what, exactly, do we to pass on? Many things, of course, including traditions, stories, wisdom, rituals – and even life itself. For Native Americans this notion of passing on includes a heavy emphasis on nature, on creation. In terms of the Fourteen Generations tradition, that means living in such a way that the seventh generations to come after you will have the same natural gifts and beauty you had.

This means living in harmony with nature. It means taking from nature only what you have to have to live. It means "walking lightly on the earth," as a Native American adage says. I saw this attitude toward nature in my mother. She used sparingly and reused long before anyone ever heard of the word "recycle." In view of the current environmental awareness, I cannot help but point out the relevance of this concern for nature. Unfortunately, the environmental awareness comes late, for much damage has been done, and it seems unlikely we will pass on to our seventh generation the same world passed on to us. The concern for nature embodied in the notion of passing on what you received strikes a religious chord as well today. It fits right in with the growing importance of creation spirituality.

Living with the Fourteen Generations is very contemporary socially and psychologically. Here I have in mind the alienation and loneliness so much a part of life today. As a child, I never experienced that, in part because I felt connected with those around me and those who came before me. I do not feel it now because I feel connected not only with those who went before me, but with those around me, as well as those who will come after me. Sadly, many people cannot say that today.

I do not offer living with Fourteen Generations as a panacea. It isn't. But it helps me to see that I am not alone and challenges me not to live only for myself. Once when I started to tell an editor about the Fourteen Generations, he said it sounded like an arithmetic lesson. No, I said, not if you add it up. If you add it up, the concept of the Fourteen Generations teaches lessons about life.

Regular Folks

39

I travel frequently in speaking around the country on prayer and spirituality. Not surprisingly, that means flying a great deal. And that means sitting next to people on planes, and, more often than not, talking to them. In these conversations, I have had one exchange countless times. It usually goes like this: People ask what I do. When I say I am a nun who teaches prayer and spirituality, they often become apologetic about what they do and say, directly or indirectly, their work lacks spiritual significance.

That response makes me sad, because it shows a failure to understand spiritual significance. These people's work may not be connected with the church, as mine, but that does not mean their work means nothing in the spiritual realm. Not knowing this, I guess, shows the sad state of spirituality among many Americans today. Lately, I have taken to doing my bit to remedy the situation. Without a lot of spiritual lingo or religious jargon, I tell my seat mates about people I come across whose work, in my judgment, reflects spiritual significance.

I tell them, for example, about the laundry man I saw at a hotel in Houston. While speaking there, I went outside one morning to meditate. I noticed the laundry man as I walked back and forth in the parking lot. He unloaded laundry – sheets, towels, pillow cases, tablecloths – from his truck onto a cart and took it into the hotel. Load after load.

Once I noticed him I found it almost impossible to continue my meditation. Finally, I decided to just watch him. That would be my morning prayer. I made a good choice, for watching him gave me much material for reflection. This man had a bounce in his step, a smile on his face. He walked with a purpose. He did not toss the laundry around. Or drop it. He set it down, often taking time to straighten an out-of-place piece. I thought of my mother making beds.

He worked efficiently, too. In 15 to 20 minutes, he brought in what looked to me like all the laundry this large hotel would need in one day. As he finished, I went over to him, said I enjoyed watching the way he worked and complimented him on his efficiency. "Lady," he said with a smile, "this hasn't got anything to do with efficiency. This is a work of art!" And, I had to agree – he worked as an artist.

Or, I will tell my fellow travelers about the guy in charge of the produce section of the Safeway where I shop. He always sprays, cleans and lines up his fruits and vegetables. He talks about them as his babies, and, indeed, he gives the impression of someone presiding over a nursery. This man loves to cook, and so do I. We started exchanging recipes. Not long ago, he gave me his recipe for "the best barbecue sauce in the world." But you must get the best ingredients, he says, adding that the right garlic becomes critical. Picking up some from the counter, he said, "These here – these are the *babies* you want." This man cares about food, and seeing to it that people get good food, more than anyone I know.

I also tell about Woody, a truck driver who lived next door when I was a child. He traveled a week or two at a time. None of us kids could wait until he got back. He brought back candy. He listened to us. He told us about his trips, making them into great adventures that appealed to us kids. For instance, he used to take us around his truck and, in great detail, tell us from which states the mud on the flaps came.

I grew up around cowboys. I remember how they cared for their horses – grooming, feeding, saddling with care, and talking to them all the while. Sometimes on the plane I talk about the cowboys. Or about policemen. The one who gave us kids rides in his motorcycle sidecar. The one who helped me get home one wintry night in Montana when my car stalled on a country road. The ones who patrol the streets of the inner city neighborhood where I live.

My traveling companions usually get the idea – doing the things regular folks do *is* spiritual, as spiritual as flying around the country teaching prayer and spirituality. I don't usually get into this on the plane, but I have never had one of these conversations without thinking about the words of Jesus in the judgment scene from twenty-fifth chapter of Matthew's gospel.

"I was tired," I can hear him saying, "and you saw to it that I had clean sheets. I was hungry, and you provided me with fresh produce. I was a child eager for adventure, and you told me stories about the world. I was growing up and impressionable, and you taught me how to care for God's creatures. I was stranded, and you gave me a lift; in danger, and you protected me."

The Iris Candle

40

In the 1970s, I lived and worked on a Sioux and Assiniboine reservation in northeastern Montana. The village in which I lived was small – about 400 – and the house I rented was also quite small. It had a medium-sized kitchen, a front room, a large closet I used as a chapel, and a tiny bedroom.

Besides my work out on the reservation, I taught catechism to children in my home, mostly in the kitchen. Because it had few cupboards and drawers, I hung many of the things you usually put in them on the walls. Walls were filled with everything from pot holders and cups to small pans and tools.

I had lots of things sitting around, too. On my desk, an old door on two sawhorses, I had all kinds of school supplies – Magic Markers, pens, colors, construction paper – and odds and ends – Band Aids, nails, candles, batteries, flashlights. Many of these things were in cups of various sizes and shapes.

One couldn't be in the kitchen without noticing all the things sitting around and hanging on the walls. That certainly was true of the kids. Sometimes, it seemed, they were more interested in what they saw than in what they heard from me. It didn't take long before they were not only looking at the things I had around the kitchen, but they were handling them, occasionally picking up an item, usually in a very loving manner, as if they wanted it.

Seeing this, I got an idea. I told the kids that on their birthdays they could have one item in my house – anything that could be seen – as a present. One Saturday, Iris, a shy but rather mature girl of 12, came to the door with her mother. "It's my birthday," she said, "and I've come to get my gift."

A new multi-colored candle got her attention. I had just received it as a gift and had put it in my little chapel. I could easily see why she would be attracted to the candle. It was eye-catching, three or four inches in diameter, a foot or so high, with so many colors that I called it my rainbow candle. But I had another candle, too, a very different one, on my desk. It was nothing but a stub, left over from the adoration chapel in the motherhouse of my community in Milwaukee. For years, I had gotten these candle stubs. I set them out in a jar lid and I would light them when I prayed. It was my way of uniting my prayer with the sisters who prayed around the clock in the chapel, as well as with the rest of my community.

I had talked about these candles during the catechism classes. It must has touched Iris because, after nearly selecting the rainbow candle, she suddenly switched her attention to this candle stub. It was no more than two inches high and so out of shape that it hardly looked like a candle anymore. She picked it up, examined it and sniffed it (it had a lovely honey-rich smell). Setting it down, she went back to the rainbow candle. Then back to the stub. Back to the rainbow. Back to the stub.

Finally, she picked up the stub and took it to her mother, indicating this was her choice. I was surprised –for this was not the candle most 12-year-olds would have chosen – and I stepped forward and said, "Iris, you are perfectly welcome to take the rainbow candle if you like." "Well," she replied, "I was going to, but I decided to take this one because it has been listening to a lot of holy thoughts." Her mother, with an approving smile, said, "Iris, you chose well."

Indeed she had. It was a choice that taught me several lessons about prayer. First, prayer takes imagination. Most children – and adults, too, for that matter – would have selected the new shiny rainbow candle as a symbol for prayer. But Iris' choice showed me that the old, the ordinary, the burnt-out, can be just as effective in aiding us in prayer. That is, if we have the imagination.

Second, we do not pray alone. For years, I had lit a candle stub to unite my prayer with that of my community, but it was only after Iris pointed out how the stubby candle had listened to many holy thoughts, that I realized how true that was. Now, the lighted candle began to symbolize not only the unity of my prayer with the present prayer of the sisters of my community, but with their prayers in the past – that is, with the "holy thoughts" it heard when they had the candle. From there, it was only a short step for me to see that my prayer was united to all prayer, past and present, not just that of my religious community. And, of course, I now see the same holds for my future prayer.

Finally, and perhaps most important: Iris said the old candle had listened to a lot of holy thoughts, a lot of prayers. As Christians, we use candles as the symbol for Christ, who is the Light of the World. From that time on, whenever I lit the candle to pray, I knew as never before that not only was the candle, the symbol, hearing my prayer, but that Christ was listening, too.

Violence Within

41

When I worked in Denver a few years ago, students at the University of Colorado, in Boulder, invited me to give a retreat on nonviolence as reflected in the writings and the lives of Martin Luther King, Jr., Mahatma Gandhi and Dorothy Day.

The drive from Denver to Boulder, on a three-lane interstate, covers a beautiful stretch. I stayed to the right so I could take my time and enjoy the mountain scenery. I came upon a young woman driving in the center lane. Even from a distance, I caught the glint of the sun on the strawberry blonde braids wrapped around her head. How striking, I thought.

Suddenly, a man, racing down an on-ramp, cut in front of me, and, just as quickly, switched to the center lane, in front of the woman driver. I could see her bristle. When he switched to the left lane, she followed, honking and giving him the finger. He switched back to the center lane. So did she, still honking, still fingering.

Not wanting to miss this little drama, I sped up, catching up as the traffic slowed them. As I did, I laughed over the absurdity of this episode, and, the next thing I knew, the woman driver gave me the finger. But her interest quickly returned to the man, and, for several miles, until he found an exit, she pursued him, switching lanes as he did, and honking until she could no longer see him.

At the retreat center, as I prepared to begin, the young woman driver walked in. She wore a dirndl skirt and peasant blouse, with sandals laced up around her calves. On her arm, she carried a knitting bag. She said to me, "Sister, I'm not making this retreat. I just came because a friend asked me. I don't need a retreat on nonviolence. I'm a potter and, you know, we potters have to have a gentle touch to work with clay. So, if you don't mind, I'll sit in the back and knit."

I assured her that would be fine. I began the retreat by saying, "A funny thing happened to me on my way here today," and I proceeded to tell the story of the highway chase in great detail (though I took care not to describe the driver). "Wow!" one man responded, "Talk about violence!" The story had such an impact on members of the group – numbering 60 or so – that they decided to discuss it, and from their comments afterward, the story brought home to them how violence lurks in all of us, how easily it can get out of control, and, perhaps most important of all, how we fail to recognize it.

The incident turned into a powerful lesson, not only for the people making the retreat but for me as well. As I think about them, King, Gandhi and Day had learned this lesson, and, I suspect, that may have been one of the reasons all three became advocates of nonviolence. King, for example, says somewhere that he choose total pacifism because he feared the violence within himself. Dorothy Day, with whom I had a number of contacts over the years, told me the same thing herself. And Gandhi urged keeping calm – maintaining an "air of peace," I believe he calls it – as a way of controlling one's own violence.

I have given many retreats over the years. I have forgotten many of them. But this one, because I learned a great lesson, stays with me. It taught me that violence goes beyond shootings in the street, blood and sex on TV and in the movies, or war. Anyone can spot that kind of violence. And denounce it.

More difficult, more subtle, I have found is the violence, or potential violence, lurking within us, within me. Unchecked, where would my raised voice lead? Or my slammed door or my tossed book? After the first session of the retreat, the woman driver came up to me and said, "Thanks for not giving me away. I think I may need this retreat, after all, because I've just found violence where I least suspected I would." She's not the only one.

To Catch a Crook

42

This is a story about the little people winning over the big, right scoring a victory over might, David beating Goliath. Actually, the story's significance extends beyond that. While at first it seems to involve only me and my effort to obtain justice for myself, I have come to see it as a story about all of us and how we work and pray for justice.

I teach in Oakland, California, where, until about six months ago, I lived in the small apartment I rented when I moved there more than three years ago. At the time I paid a $650 deposit that the landloard would return when I left. I enjoyed the apartment the first couple of years but drug dealers took over the neighborhood, and, with some reluctance, I decided to move because I no longer felt safe.

I notified the landlord. He checked out the apartment to make sure I had not done any damage. He did not find any. He said he would return my deposit in a week or so, as required by law. But it never came. After a couple weeks, I started checking. And – surprise! – the landlord had disappeared. No longer at his old address. No new address. Phone disconnected. No new number.

I had been ripped off. I contacted the police. They said they did not have enough evidence, even though I had a copy of the lease. I fumed for a few days, trying to figure out how to track down this guy and get my money back. It would not be easy. I had nothing to go on, plus nothing to go in – I don't have a car.

But I needed the money. Since I don't own a car, I ride cabs some. I had gotten to know one driver in particular, Ade Odunikan, a Nigerian, who had given me rides and who had always been helpful. I asked him to come by, saying I had a proposition for him. If he would help me catch this crook and get my deposit back I would give him part of it. His wide smile gave his answer.

The next morning we got into his cab. We checked the police, telephone company, post office. Nothing. We drove around the area where the landlord used to live. I remembered he had a fancy car, a Jaguar. We looked for that. No luck. We asked people on the street if they had seen the man or the car. Still nothing. Once in a while, when we did not know what else to do, Ade and I said a prayer.

Then we got a break. We found an auto repair place that had done work on his car. He had a place somewhere in the hills east of the city, they said. We headed that way. Soon, we entered the next county. We decided to head for the courthouse. Yes, he had a place way up in the hills. Paid taxes on it. We set out for it on hilly, curvy, dusty, narrow, unmarked roads.

I don't know how many wrong turns we made. We made a couple more prayer stops. Then I saw the Jaguar parked in front of a house. We knocked on the door. He would not come out and denied being my landlord or knowing me. We went back to the courthouse, to see the sheriff. We got a cold reception. We, the cabbie and I – a black and a woman –had run into the good old boy network, the one made up of whites and males. But I argued and threatened until the sheriff went out to the landlord's place with us, where, eventually, we got a check for $650. We hurried back to town and cashed it before the landlord stopped payment.

I learned two lessons from this experience. First, all of us little people must work together to obtain justice. We must have compassion for each other. We must trust each other. We must share what we have. Ade and I did that. He had compassion. He trusted me. I shared the deposit with him. Together, we got justice – and enriched each other.

The second lesson – related to the first – concerns the way we pray. When we prayed during our search, Ade and I said the usual prayers of petition one would say in a situation like that, "God, help us find this guy so that we can get my money back," etc. Often, when we say prayers such as this, we sound as if we are asking God, and only God, to do what we ask – to get a job for us, to help the poor, to get our money back.

But our payer must not end there. We also must do our part. We must act. We must take the steps necessary to bring about the desired result. That means when we say prayers of petition we are not only asking God to act, we also ask God to help us act. In effect, we ask God to change us – in this case, we did not ask that God somehow magically lead us to the landlord, but that God give us the strength and the courage to persevere.

We could have been discouraged at the beginning when we had nothing to go on and our search did not turn up anything. We could have given up when lost in the hills. We could have backed down when the sheriff let us know his sympathies did not lie with a woman and a black man from the next county over. But we did not. In part, I believe that resulted from our prayer asking for the courage to act.

One more point: We must not limit this prayer for the courage to act to instances when we need help, when we suffer. We must pray this way when other people are in need, when other people hurt. This last point makes finding my landlord and getting my money back a story about how all of us must work and pray for justice.

43

My Walkabout

The aborigines of Australia have a custom called a walkabout. They make it a kind of pilgrimage from one holy place to another and it serves as a break from their normal activities. I have developed my own version of a walkabout. The aborigines do their walkabouts in the bush country where they live. I do mine in urban America – in the multiracial section of the city of Oakland where I live. Like the aborigines, I use it as a break, too – actually, I have turned it into a prayer break.

I make mine an early morning walkabout. It serves as a way of exercising my body and keeping it fit. Once, back in the old days, we thought of exercise as only that, a way of keeping the body fit. But these days, we understand the wholeness of things better, and I see keeping physically fit connects with keeping spiritually fit.

As soon as I step out my door, a second spiritual characteristic of my walkabout becomes evident – I move out into my community. Once, again back in the old days, many of us tended to limit spirituality to our own relationship to God. Often other people did not have much to do with it. But we cannot get by with that today. Among other things, liberation theology and the biblical emphasis on covenant prevent that.

Right outside my door, as I write this, two mourning doves nest in a tree. They become my first stop. Each morning I feed them. Since two fat cats live in the neighborhood, I serve as lookout as well as provider. Each time, this reminds me that we must not only feed each other, but look out for each other. What could be more basic to Christianity? Further, as a Franciscan, feeding the birds puts me in touch with my roots and St. Francis' love of all God's creatures.

Flowers bloom in California all year around. In the summer, they display every color, and brilliantly. But the beauty of the morning goes beyond what I see on the ground. Before sunrise, the sky glows, and, as it brightens, I often sense it revealing more than light.

Old houses abound in my neighborhood. Once rather grand, in many cases they have become apartments. Often I think of the families who lived and loved in them. Imagine all the joys and the sorrows people experienced in these old homes. Somehow, as a believer in an incarnational God, I know God participated in all of it. Further, I believe God still does so today with the people who live in them now.

Soon after I begin my walkabout, people start coming out and heading for work, first one, then three or four, then a steady stream. All go to earn the money to buy the food and to provide the shelter for loved ones who would otherwise be hungry and homeless. The scene evokes countless scripture passages, including a favorite of mine, the judgment scene in Matthew's gospel, in which Jesus says, "I was hungry and you gave me to eat."

Garbage pick-up takes place on Tuesday. The men work quickly, and as a team, anticipating each other's moves in bringing the garbage from the curb and moving the truck along the street. Friendly as well as efficient, they take time to wave or to chat. They strike me as the type Jesus associated with – poor, looked down upon, without influence. Since he mingled with this type once, I expect he does so today as well.

I find Saturday the most interesting day. On Saturday, people set out items that can be recycled for pick-up – paper, plastic, bottles, cans. They use yellow, laundry-like baskets. As soon as the yellow baskets appear, so do the people I call "the shoppers," because of the way they use old grocery carts. They pick out what they can sell, put it in the carts, and haul it off. I have gotten to know a few of these shoppers. One, an 80-year-old woman, says she does it to supplement her meager Social Security check. Several families come regularly. Their kids stamp cans flat so they can haul more at one time. For Mrs. Kell, a single mother of two, this type of shopping does not differ much from her regular job – shopping for four or five shut-ins at nearby stores. She does that with a grocery cart, too.

I see recycling as the high point of my walkabout. While many of the things provide reminders of God's presence and the way God wants us to live, none does it quite as well as recycling. In recycling, people not only cooperate, but they demonstrate a special awareness that creation and all things in it come from God as gifts.

While my walkabout differs in many ways from that of the aborigines – the setting being a major one – I see similarities, too. The most important: Like the aborigines, I have come to see my walkabout as a pilgrimage from one holy place to another.

The Land I Love

44

I have always loved this land. I have traveled all across it. I have spoken in every state, including Alaska and Hawaii, and lived in more states than I can count without making a concentrated effort. I have loved every place I have been, some more than others, of course, and I have never been any place where I didn't feel at home.

My love affair with the land began in southern Colorado, where I grew up. We lived in the desert, which spread out to the south. To the north we looked up to the San Juan mountains, which rose to heights of more than 13,000 feet.

From the desert, I learned not to take the land for granted. At first the desert seems unable to sustain life. Little seems to happen. Life is sparse, growth slow, the change of seasons subtle. Life in the desert seems precarious, as if hanging by a thread. From my earliest days I remember feeling that, as Native Americans say, "we must walk lightly upon the land." Growing up in the desert, I learned I must love the land tenderly.

Mountains taught me a different love of the land. As a child we went to the mountains to play and to hunt. As an adult I lived all along the Continental Divide, from Arizona to Montana. While working in Montana, I frequently drove the 100 miles from Great Falls to Helena alone. Sometimes I would recite lines from the psalms that came to me, "Praise the Lord, all you hills, praise the Lord, all you mountains. Praise the Lord, you holy frost, praise the Lord, all you snows." In time I got so I thought of the trip as living the psalms. Not only was I saying the psalms, the beautiful mountains around me seemed to be say them right back at me.

From the mountains, both as a child and as an adult, I learned that, in contrast to the desert, the land is powerful and majestic. As a child playing in the mountains, I sensed we were in a land made by One greater than we are. As an adult I became convinced of it, especially while making that trip from Great Falls to Helena. As a result I learned that we could love the Lord by loving the land.

In the farmland of the Midwest, I learned the opposite lesson – that God can love us through the land. I went to the Midwest after entering the Sisters of St. Francis, in Milwaukee. Because I had a driver's license, a rare thing among sisters in those days, I frequently served as a driver for the head of the community and her counsel.

As a result, I became familiar with the Wisconsin countryside, where I saw cows in rich pastures, and fields green with corn and hay – all sources of food for us. It didn't take me long to learn to love the land in the Midwest, especially after I discovered the cranberries of northern Wisconsin and Michigan and the blueberries in upper Minnesota.

When I lived in the east, mostly around Boston, I learned to love it, too. I would drive up north to see the maple trees tapped. In the fall, the trees of New England, as everyone knows, turn to colors beyond description. The trees' spring color is more subtle. It took a poet, Robert Frost, to capture that. He wrote, "Nature's first green is gold/ her hardest hue to hold/ her early leaf a flower/ but only so an hour." Those lines capture the way willow trees develop in the spring. They come out in a pale gold, but stay that color only a week or so before turning a deeper green.

Last Thanksgiving I had dinner with one of my old college friends, a woman I've kept in touch with over the years. She put on a wonderful feast for a rather large gathering, about 30 people. During the meal we got talking about the origin of the foods we were eating. My friend, knowing of my interest in the subject, asked me to tell the group what I knew. I went down the line: Turkey, sweet potatoes, cranberries, squash, pumpkin (for the pie), and corn (for the corn bread) all are native to this country. As it turned out, just about everything on our table originated here. Further, Native Americans brought most of these foods to the colonists when they shared their first Thanksgiving meals.

As we approach Thanksgiving again, and I reflect on the land I love, it becomes increasingly clear why I love it: From my earliest days in the desert, to the heights of the mountains, to the staples of the Midwest, to the beauties of the Northeast, and to the abundance on my table, it has loved me first.

45

I have never owned a camera. Yet, because people have given me pictures over the years I have managed to collect enough photographs to make my old album fat. I like putting new pictures into the album. I like looking at the pictures. And, for some years now, I have liked praying over it.

My photo album has become one of my favorite prayer books. Three or four times a year I get it out, not only to look and to reminisce, but to pray. I do a lot of remembering and reliving as the photos bring back memory after memory of people, places and events. But I don't stop there. Almost automatically I find myself becoming aware of the fact that God is present in these pictures. Of course I see God only with the eyes of faith, but God's presence is real nevertheless. And this same faith tells me God is present with me as well, as I look and reminisce with the photos. And as I pray.

Sometimes I never get past the opening page. There I have three prints and a tintype, which is a thin metal sheet with an image. The prints depict Our Lady of Guadeloupe, St. Francis of Assisi, and Blessed Kateri Tekakwitha. All three are religious ideals of mine. All three reflect God's work in a way that means much to me.

As the child of a Native American mother, I have always loved the story of Our Lady of Guadalupe. To me, her appearance to Juan Diego, a Mexican peasant, serves as a reminder of God's presence and activity among the native poor of this continent. The same with Blessed Kateri Tekakwitha, the first North American Indian candidate for canonization. St. Francis represents two streams of spirituality vitally important to me: that of my Franciscan religious community and the sacredness of creation.

But it is the tintype, an old bent one, that has produced some of my deepest prayer. It depicts my grandmother pregnant with my mother. In giving it to me years ago, my mother said, "I'm in this picture, right in the middle of her." Years later, I would be "in the middle of my mother" in the same way she was in the middle of her mother in this tintype. Thus, in looking at this image, I am looking at the source of my life. And that means that God is present in it, too.

The first one-third of the album contains old black and white snapshots. There's one of my dear old friend from high school, Naomi. She was a beautiful girl, and I envied her. She always called me "Shidoni," which means "friend" in Navajo. At the time I was having a hard time seeing anything beautiful about myself. Reflecting with my photo album helped me to believe and to accept that I was eminently worthwhile.

Three of my closest friends from college are dead. One from cancer, one from suicide over a lover, and I don't know how the third died. Then there is Betty. We have kept in touch all these years. I have seen her children grow up. She's a grandmother now. A year ago we celebrated Thanksgiving together. I have spent a lot of time with these college pictures. Perhaps it is because that is the time when we separate from our parents and begin to struggle with life on our own. As I reflect on these struggles, I become more and more persuaded God participates in them as well, suffering with us in our losses, celebrating with us in our victories.

Then there are the convent pictures. These indeed were formative years, with great spiritual leaders and mystics – Sister Mary Esther, Sister Romuald, Sister Doris H., Sister Julian, Sister Mary Alacoque, and others like Sisters Dorothy, Cordé, Margery, Pat and Betty. Sister Mary Esther stands out. I could not spend afternoons in the convent backyard with her without believing in God's presence there with us. Eventually such experiences helped me to see God's presence not only in the convent backyard but in all backyards.

110

Among the color pictures, two of Native American children have become my favorites for reflection. One shows a dozen or so sitting on my porch on a cold snowy day when I lived in Montana. They used to wait for me to come home. I would invite them in and we would have hot chocolate and cookies around the kitchen table. Usually I would end up telling them stories. The picture serves as a nice reminder of what we can do when we get together around a table and share stories and food.

In the other picture, children are dancing. I saw these youngsters in Oregon. They had their moccasins on and they were doing really fancy footwork. People were taking pictures. I asked the children if they would pick out one and send it to me, because I thought their dancing was great. Later, when the picture came, it showed only feet – no heads, no arms, just feet! For them, that was the most important, and they did not want me to miss it. I smile whenever I look at that picture. Invariably, too, it brings on reflection about the mystical body of Christ.

Often we equate praying with saying words. My experience with my photo album shows that pictures can provide a meaningful way to pray, too. Which raises the question, when it comes to prayer, is the old saying true? Is a picture worth a thousand words? I say at least. I am even tempted to go out and buy a camera.

Letters for Lent

46

Nearly thirty years ago I was traveling in Minnesota visiting two young women who had expressed interest in entering my religious community. I was near St. Cloud when a terrific snowstorm hit. "Stay off the roads," the radio warned. Since I had friends in a nearby monastery, I decided to stop and ask them for shelter. They had an empty guest house apart from the convent and offered it to me – for a week or so if I liked. I decided this would be a good opportunity for a private retreat, so I called home and got permission to stay.

Just the week before I had been reading the book of Revelation and had thought how the section on the Letters to the Churches (chapters two and three) could be a good basis for a retreat or an intensive examination of conscience. Now, I had the time and the place.

I was right. The letters did make for a good examen and retreat. After eight days I left renewed. Since then, I have offered the idea to others, who also have reported positive results. In recent years, I have suggested that reflection on the letters as a good way for making Lent, and, with Ash Wednesday coming up, I suggest it again now.

From that first retreat, I remember so well the big and bold images used in introducing each of the letters. They are like grand skywriting. There are the Seven Stars, Seven Golden Lampstands, Two-Edged Swords, Blazing Eyes and Shining Feet, Seven Spirits, Key of David and the Amen. Each refers to Christ, and just reflecting on these references and their meaning could make for a good retreat or a good Lent.

Since that retreat, I have compared several scriptural translations – New English, Revised Standard, New Jerusalem,

J.B. Phillips, and a recent presentation titled The Message, by Eugene H. Peterson. Of them, I like Phillips best. It is very readable, yet the translator does not impose his personality on the text. In addition, the translation's headings help to focus each letter's emphasis.

The first letter is to the church at Ephesus. Phillips' heading refers to it as the Loveless Church. Like most of the letters, it praises strengths, good deeds, and admirable qualities. And then comes the whammy! "I hold this against you. . . ." The people are chastised because, in spite of their good words, they love less now than they once did. They are called upon to repent or else the lampstand (signifying Christ's presence) will be removed.

The letter to the Persecuted Church (Smyrna) is essentially positive. It encourages the people to be strong and to persevere, and reminds them that they are not alone. In letters to the Over-Tolerant (Pergamum) and Compromising (Thyatira) churches, suspicions are raised about dedication and whole-heartedness, about the lack of willingness to take a stand on things that matter. Don't rock the boat. Keep peace at any price, even if superficial.

The basically positive letter to the Church with Opportunity (Philadelphia) is inspiring. The writer points out to members of this church that when doors were opened to them (that is, opportunities to share the faith), they did not close them, even if the doors were only open a crack. They seized opportunities and acted on them. They are assured of support and care.

The strongest words are directed at the Sleeping Churches (Sardis) and the Complacent Church (Laodicea). The Sleeping Church passes for being alive, but the writer's judgment is otherwise: "You have a reputation for being alive, but, in fact, you are dead. Wake up! Strengthen what you still have, before it too dies."

The Complacent Church receives the harshest criticism and the most pleading invitation. The words are also the best known: "I know what you have done, and that you are neither cold nor hot. I could wish that you were either cold or hot! But since you are lukewarm, neither hot nor cold, I intend to vomit you out of my mouth. While you say, 'I am rich, I have prospered, there is nothing I need,' you have no eyes to see what a wretched, pitiable poverty-stricken, blind and naked creature you are."

These hard words are spoken by The Amen, a description of the exalted Christ as "the faithful and true witness, the source of God's creation." But then he changes his tone and reminds the members of the necessity of correcting their ways and that repentance is the way to real growth. Then he utters some of the most consoling words in all of scripture, "Behold, I stand knocking at your door."

I think you can see the potential these letters hold for examination and reflection. Just for starters there's not loving enough, compromising, being overly tolerant of untruth, sleeping instead of being vigilant, complacency. These are bracing propositions. Not ones we want to face, for they call for repentance and for correcting our ways. Each of the seven letters concludes with this refrain, "Let the listener hear what the Spirit says to the churches." In other words, these are words for each of us. They are words from the Spirit. If we listen, if we examine ourselves, if we mend our ways, I am sure we also will hear the same reassuring words the complacent Christians of Laodicea heard from The Amen, "Behold, I stand knocking at your door."

47

Wild air, world-mothering air,
Nestling me everywhere,
That each eyelash or hair
Girdles;

I first read these lines from Gerard Manly Hopkins' poem, "The Blessed Virgin Compared to the Air We Breathe," years ago while walking on the campus of Notre Dame. I was thrilled. And still am.

This time of year we are concerned about fresh air. Springtime is about fresh air. New ideas are about freshness and creativity. So it seems that springtime – a time when we become doubly aware of motherhood – is a good time to reflect on this abundance.

The earth yields sprouts and buds and shoots and grasses, mothering new life. Birth is all around us. This makes me think of the mothers who nurture, the men who nurture, all of us who bring life into the world.

Three women from the scriptures come especially to mind – Sarah, Elizabeth, and Mary.

Sarah and Abraham, her husband, were both advanced in age, and together had no child. Abraham was visited by three young men, one of whom told him Sarah would bear a son. Sarah, listening behind the tent, laughed. Not only was Abraham old, but she was far too old for children. And yet the prophecy came true. The visitor said, "In the spring we shall return and Sarah shall have a child." She did have a child, and they named that child Isaac, which means "God laughs."

Elizabeth and Zachariah were also childless. The scriptures say they, like Abraham and Sarah, were advanced in years and that Elizabeth was barren. Nevertheless, Zachariah received a message in the temple from an angel, Gabriel, that Elizabeth would have a son who would be called John. This was John the Baptist. Zachariah was struck dumb, but Elizabeth conceived.

Six months later, Mary was approached by Gabriel and told of her place in salvation. She received the news and went quickly to visit Elizabeth, her cousin. When they met, the child in Elizabeth's womb leapt. There was birth. There was youth. There was age. And there was vitality.

In these three episodes, we have birth in an old woman, in a barren woman, and in a young virgin. All three were most unlikely vessels for such favoritism from God. This makes me think of our excuses for not being fruitful, for not being productive, for not being men and women who give life, who give birth. These days we seem so eager to find a scapegoat, for someone or something to blame for our personal infertility.

"Don't blame me," we say, "I'm too old. At my age you can't expect me to be excited and interested in things. I can't keep producing at my age. Just too old."

Or: "Don't blame me for my infertility. I had a bad childhood. Lots of things have gone wrong in my life. I never really had a chance like most people. Too many strikes against me. I'm not responsible. Don't blame me that I am not life-giving and vital."

Or: "I'm too young, you know. I haven't had all the experience the rest of you have had. I need a lot more years before you can have such great expectations of me. Give me time, give me time. I am too young to be productive. I have to take care of myself."

I see one great difference between the three women of the scripture who gave life and the excuses I hear so often today about not being able to do so. The women of scripture encountered God and responded in faith. Perhaps all three of these women call us to a faith response, to the power of the Holy Spirit to make great things happen in us and through us.

The great artist Grandma Moses and the great saint Teresa of Avila both got off to a rather late start, and yet wonderful beauty and marvelous insight and vision happened through these two women. They were responsive. They were fertile in the Spirit. They were fertile in creativity, hopefulness and faith.

116

We are not too old. We are not too young. We are not too impotent, too bound by circumstances to make a difference, to call ourselves and others to life. We can hear the call, the word of God, and do as Jesus asked us to do – act on the word. We may all be in the fiat posture of Mary, "Be it done unto me according to thy word." And then others will ask of us, as Gerard Manley Hopkins asked in awe of the season of spring, "What is all this juice and all this joy?"

48

Waving Good News

I suppose the first thing I should tell you about this man is that he is not a nut. I want to make that clear immediately because the thing he did was different – so different that on first hearing you might very well wonder, "Is this guy crazy?"

So, what did he do? Every morning he went out in front of his house and waved to people. For an hour and a half or so. According to news stories, he did it for 33 years. What's more, he did it in Berkeley, California, a city that has been in the news its share of times for things unusual.

Now you see why I started by saying he is not a nut. And he isn't. People love him for what he did. Especially children. Several times, according to news accounts, when the school system planned to reroute buses that passed his house, children protested until the proposed changes were canceled.

Adults liked him too. Like the children, they returned his waves and sometimes stopped to chat. All of this got him a certain amount of recognition. The Berkeley Chamber of Commerce thought so much of what he did that it gave him its community service award. That's when I heard about him, first on the local news – I live in neighboring Oakland – and then on national television. He struck me as someone special and so I called him. Among other things, I said that, as a teacher of prayer and spirituality, I thought that what he did was not only Christian, but could even be thought of as a form of prayer.

"You got it, Sister, you got it," he said. "That's what I am doing. I wave to the people. I smile for them. That's really my prayer for them. Everything they hear on the news is bad. I just want them to have one good moment. That's what I am trying to do."

He told me his name was Joseph, but said he did not want his last name used because he did not want to draw attention to himself. An African-American, Joseph, the father of five children, is now in his 80s and retired. Before retiring, he said he did his waving before going to work busing dishes in a restaurant.

I bring Joseph to your attention because I think he teaches all of us about what it means not only to be human, but to be Christian. It strikes me, first, that he is a good reminder that all of us have gifts – regardless of who we are or where we are. He is obviously an ordinary man, a man with little education, with a job that was nothing special. He carried out the important task – and Christian vocation – of raising a family. In other words, he was what you might call a solid citizen type. But he went beyond that, reaching out to one and all, to people he knew and didn't know, trying, as he said, to provide them with a "good moment."

Second, Joseph did not wait around for someone else – an expert or someone in authority – to tell him what to do or when and where to do it. Instead, he saw something that he thought needed doing – to provide a little good news – and he did it.

Third, he did it right where he lives. In the front yard of his nondescript house, before leaving for his nondescript job. In that, I think he teaches an especially important lesson to us as Christians, because we often think that we could do great things if we weren't tied down to ordinary lives in ordinary places.

Fourth, and this may be one of his most important lessons, he teaches us a lot about perseverance. Imagine, coming out on your front lawn and waving to people for 33 years! At times, I suspect, he must have wondered just how much good he was doing. Some people who passed him no doubt did think he was crazy. But he persevered, doing what he, and only he, believed worthwhile.

Fifth, he did something that all of us as Christians must do before we can have an impact: He read the signs of the times. When I asked him why he was doing it, he immediately said it was because everywhere all the time people were being bombarded by bad news. They had too many bad moments. As he looked at their situation, he saw they needed a good moment. And he proceeded to provide one.

I grew up in rural areas of the southwestern United States. In meeting there, people spoke to each other, waved to each other. Although I have lived in urban areas for many years, I still have not gotten used to the fact that people in cities today meet each other without the slightest nod or wave. When someone like Joseph comes along – and does nod and wave, I feel the need to assure you that he is not a nut.

Perhaps that says something about the rest of us.

Christmas Presents:
Good Men

49

"It's not the men in my life that count,
It's the life in my men!"
—Mae West

The other day a friend sent me a card with this note: "When I saw this, I thought of you and all the good men that have been in your life for years." It's true, and it fits. My friends, both men and women, have a way of lasting – through hard times and easy, through nearness and distance. I've mentioned a number of my favorite women in articles, but I've never written specifically of the men – until now. These men I've known longer than fifteen years, and though we may not see each other often, the friendships hold. Such gifts of inspiration, influence, concern, and delight they have been.

Besides my father and brothers, I go way back to Father Joe Lane. He was our first priest in the desert, a Jesuit sent to the Southwest because he had tuberculosis. He was my inspiration to become a priest and my model for preaching, and he was my first experience of the wonderful Irish.

My first year in college I met Father Bob Hoffman, our Newman Club director. He opened doors to many worlds – spiritual, intellectual and social. That was 47 years ago, and we're still good friends. Bob lives and works in Denver, a local call from the airport whenever I pass through on my frequent travels.

Most of my men friends are Brothers or Priests, because we share the same work and visions. Brother David Steindl-Rast introduced me to Henri Nouwen and Thomas Berry. We've met in many different places over the years; Henri is in Canada, Tom nas moved to North Carolina after many years in New York City, and David is at Big Sur right here in California. My good friends Thomas Clarke, S.J., Jim (Martin) Clark, OFM Cap., and Michael Warren all live near New York City. I keep in touch because I travel to the East frequently.

My work with Native peoples has brought some very special men into my life: Father Pete Guthneck (Montana), Joe and Fr. Ed Savilla (New Mexico), Bishop Tom Murphy (Seattle), Fr. Diego Mazon, OFM (New Mexico), and Fr. Stan Nadolny (Arizona).

Education and spiritual growth areas have given me Fr. Tom Cahalane, Bishop Joseph Green (recently deceased), and Jerry Villano – all of Tucson. Abbot Emmanuel (Joe Spillane), Richard Rohr, Don Fischer, Msgr. Bob Fox (deceased), Matthew Fox, Joe Dillon, Joe Miller – all these are men I have been able to turn to at times of need. Art Winter, former editor of *Praying* magazine, and Clink Thomson, director of Credence Cassettes, have been steady helps and friends.

I've laughed and cried with these men, learned from them and grown through them. Just to call them to mind is a litany of thanksgiving. ¡Olé! And Deo Gratias!